Secrets of the Body:
Your Character and Future Revealed
Jocelyne Cooke

The ancient Chinese recognized the fact that no two people are identical. Differences can be small and subtle, or very obvious. Some people are long-limbed, others are heavy-set. Height and weight come in myriad variations. Facial features make each person in the world unique.
Jocelyn Cooke explains how our bodies contain numerous secrets about our character and future, which we can learn to decipher. With the help of this book, you will understand the significance of the color, texture, shape, and size of your various organs and features.

Jocelyne Cooke lives in Sydney. In the early 1980s, she visited the Philippines, Hong Kong, China, and Japan, and met up with people who were interested in various mystical methods of character analysis and predicting the future. She was fascinated by the Chinese method of "reading" the body and the face, and she spent several years in the Far East perfecting the arts. She then went to Los Angeles, and, after a three-year stay, returned to Australia, where she practices these arts.
Jocelyne Cooke is also the author of "Secrets of the Face: Your Character and Future Revealed."

ASTROLOG COMPLETE GUIDES SERIES

Jocelyne Cooke

Secrets of the
BODY

Your Character and Future Revealed

Astrolog Publishing House

Astrolog Publishing House
P. O. Box 1123, Hod Hasharon 45111, Israel
Tel: 972-9-7412044
Fax: 972-9-7442714
E-Mail: info@astrolog.co.il
Astrolog Web Site: www.astrolog.co.il

ISBN 965-494-101-5

Published by Astrolog Publishing House 2000

Printed in Israel
10 9 8 7 6 5 4 3 2 1

Introduction

As human beings, we may not have any control over our births or deaths, but we do have the possibility of directing our lives, developing our talents and shaping our bodies. While none of us has complete control over the direction of our lives, we do have the power to influence - to a certain extent - our own lives or those of people close to us, such as our children. To this end we must become totally familiar with our bodies and the possibilities that are open to us.

The aim of this book is to teach the reader the factors that influence man's existence - how they manifest themselves via the body's secrets, and how they can be utilized for improving physical development in order to be healthy. These factors can also be used for enhancing personality and character traits, as well as shaping the individual. In this way, the person's economic basis and status can be influenced while he is maturing, and he can even ensure quality aging, as well as the preservation of a youthful spirit. Not only is it possible, but it is mandatory to improve the individual's life, to shape his path and to help him cope with the quirks of fate, all the while providing him with suitable tools to improve his physical abilities and mental capacity so that he can live and age in contentment and good health.

While the study of the body's structure and the functioning of its parts indicates the ideal and the reality, and provides tools for improvement, it will also enhance the individual's life, and help him achieve what he was destined to achieve.

The Chinese sages - the wise men of the East - discerned that what they called "the meeting between heaven and earth" existed in the human body, and noted the influence of the cosmic energies flowing in the universe on the human body, when the active energy, Yang - the male energy - and the passive, receptive energy, Yin - the female energy - flow through the human body along defined channels called *meridians* in varying degrees of intensity. The strength of the energy operating in the various regions of the body is what regulates the body's functioning, as well as the improvement of the functioning according to what is required.

Both the physical capabilities of the person and his mental ability and specific talents can be analyzed in accordance with the amount of energies that are present in the body. Moreover, the correct study of the human body can provide the appropriate tools for improving the person's physical, emotional and mental characteristics. The way to do this is to balance the cosmic energies in the body, the aim being to create a harmony between the body and the energies. As a result, the person's accomplishments will be impressive, his health excellent, and his quality of life good.

The analysis of the body in its entirety is the first stage in the study of the body's secrets, according to the view of the ancient East. After a comprehensive examination, every part of the body can be investigated, the final aim of which is the precise analysis of the organs, so as to indicate the body's strengths and weaknesses. By becoming acquainted with the characteristics, the person can improve and enhance quality of life via accurate self-assessment, and learning and practicing ways of improvement.

The improvement of one's life can begin on the physical and health plane and continue to the mental or emotional plane. The business and social planes can also benefit - in fact every aspect of life can be influenced, on condition that the energies are utilized appropriately and to the correct extent, bringing about equilibrium and the desired result.

Sometimes external aids are required to encourage the desired result - equilibrium. These aids can take the form of physical or mental exercises, or correct nutrition - all of which aim to improve the inner equilibrium of the body.

The traditional Chinese reading of the body is based on eight main topics. The division into eight is a key division in Chinese mysticism. It should be remembered that in the *I Ching* or in the Feng Shui method, there is a division into eight trigrams or the eight winds of the heavens.

The first topic deals with the basic analysis of the person. This analysis is performed according to the five Chinese elements which regulate the existence of the world: wood, fire, earth, water and metal (sometimes gold replaces metal).

Wood is a symbol of wisdom and multifariousness, fire is a symbol of glory, the earth that stores resources within itself is a symbol of security, water is a symbol of wealth, and metal is a symbol of equilibrium.

Most people contain the characteristics of several elements within them. What determines their characteristics depends on the amount of the different elements present. The balance between the combination of these elements ultimately determines their nature.

People whose element is pure, rather than a combination of elements, are considered to be the most successful expression of their element.

The second topic deals with Yang and Yin - the active and passive energies that are found in the body. When there is a balance between the two types of energy, the person enjoys an ideal life, since his physical build is perfect and his emotional and intellectual characteristics are also influenced by the appropriate energies.

The third topic deals with the balance among physical build, the intellect and the soul. When there is an equal division of energies among these three factors, the person tends toward perfection. When the equality is disrupted, positive and negative characteristics are formed, according to the extent of the influence of the particular factor.

The fourth topic deals with the location of the parts of the body, and with their influence on the person's characteristics.

(In the West, the corresponding preoccupation occurs with the sizes of the body parts and their proportion to one another.)

The correct location indicates positive characteristics, health and strength.

The fifth topic deals with the shaping of the person's appearance, voice and gait. Is he irascible? Does he conduct himself with restraint and self-control? Is his voice ringing and clear? Is his gait heavy or light?

By extension, whether a person is accepted in society can be determined via his appearance; by analyzing the kind of voice he has and its strength, it is possible to assess the extent of his self-confidence and the weight of his character.

The sixth topic deals with the complexion of the skin, which is also a distinguishing factor in the analysis of the person. Sparkling eyes indicate curiosity, smooth skin radiates inner warmth and empathetic feelings. A healthy complexion reflects a determined nature, and skin color is also significant in character analysis. For instance, facial skin that is darker than the skin covering the rest of the body attests to a person with positive qualities.

The seventh topic, which deals with the examination of the parts of the human body, is also a topic which permits the assessment of the person's limitations and advantages. For example, a broad male chest is an indication of strength and self-confidence.

The eighth topic, which deals with the examination of the person's soul, is important and must be related to. External ugliness fades away when the soul is beautiful or good, since goodness of heart is also reflected in the person's external appearance, and in most cases obliterates external ugliness.

Myriad factors combine in the creation of each person's essence, factors which vary from person to person, thus creating the differences between the various types.

The detailed ancient Chinese method of examining the body is timeless, and what was correct and appropriate thousands of years ago is also applicable to life today. Moreover, our modern lifestyle, which is characterized by its fast pace and competitiveness, would benefit from a pause for studying and examining the ideal and the reality, so that we can improve it and make the most of the little things we are inclined to forget about.

CHAPTER ONE

THE HUMAN BODY IN ITS ENTIRETY

Although we all know our bodies to a greater or lesser extent - their shortcomings as well as the parts we think should be emphasized - it would seem that the connection between the body's dimensions and proportions and the personality has not been sufficiently researched, so that people are generally unaware that success in life is linked to their body's dimensions, proportions and build.

Ancient Chinese theories state unequivocally that inherent in a person's physical build are the fundamentals of his behavior, success, and activity. Therefore, the study of a person's physical build can enable the necessary improvements to be made, which will result in social and economic success, and so on.

The ancient Chinese distinguished five types of physical build, which derived from the five elements in the cosmic structure, each of which in turn is linked to one of the five planets known at the time.

Structural characteristics and color were added to each type, as can be seen in the chart below:

Element	Planet	Shape	Color
Fire	Mars	Triangle	Red
Wood	Jupiter	Inverted triangle	Green
Metal	Venus	Rectangle	White
Water	Star (Mercury)	Circle	Black
Earth	Saturn	Square	Golden brown

From this chart, a basic human form can be constructed using fundamental characteristics which are supported by the stars and reflect human vitality.

The five elements that constitute the various types are found in different combinations in every human being. The reason for the vast differences that exist between people, both in physical build and intellectual and emotional characteristics, resides in the strength and weight of each component in the particular individual.

Physical Build	Slim, muscular	Tall, angular	Balanced	Fat	Solid
Planet	Mars	Jupiter	Venus	Star (Mercury)	Saturn
Element	Fire	Wood	Metal	Water	Earth
Body Shape	Triangle	Inverted triangle	Rectangle	Circle	Square
Complexion	Reddish	Olive	Ivory	Dark	Yellow brown
Temperament	Active	Spaced out	Pleasant	Flexible	Quiet
Future	Fame	Wisdom	Status	Wealth	Confidence
Field	Adventures	Science, Art	Management	Finance	Industry

11

The number of people who have a single, pure element is small. Most people tend to have a range of elements within them. Although each person has one predominant element, the influence of other elements is recognized. Color and complexion are factors that appear in different types. It is worth noting that every combination exerts an influence on character traits and intellect, and the combination of the elements creates the ultimate form of the particular person.

Each type is linked mainly to one of the five elements. There are elements that either help other elements or are helped by other elements during the combination of the characteristics of one element with those of another:

	Fire	**Wood**	**Metal**	**Water**	**Earth**
Helps	Earth	Fire	Water	Wood	Metal
Is helped by	Wood	Water	Earth	Metal	Fire
Inhibits	Metal	Earth	Wood	Fire	Water
Is inhibited by	Water	Metal	Fire	Earth	Wood

It is worth noting that a combination (such as marriage) consisting of people of the same type is not recommended, because instead of helping each other, there are liable to be conflicts between them, while combinations consisting of different types will inspire the ones who are strong in their field to help their partners who are weak in that field - and vice versa.

The average type of person, as we mentioned before, contains a combination of various characteristics within him, and for that reason, a relationship with a partner expands the range of possible combinations between them.

Fire Types

General remarks

Fire people are tall, thin, strong, muscular, and energetic. Their muscles are light, which means that they are not heavy people, but strong, with smooth, taut, youthful skin. They are healthy in mind and spirit, and consequently, they can be assured of success in life: They will be wealthy, famous and long-lived. The dynamic which rules their lives is quick, catalyzing their development. They are natural adventurers who enjoy flaunting their triumphs.

The **physical build** of fire people is triangular - broad at the base and narrowing as it goes upward toward their pointed heads; this shape is reminiscent of fire, which is their dominant element. They are generally high-waisted, and women of the fire type usually have small, upright breasts. (This physical build is seen mainly in "pure" fire types.)

Fire people's **heads** are pointed at the top and broad at the base. At the sides of the head, it is difficult to discern bones. Their foreheads are curved. The base of the back of their head is characterized by a protuberance, which is an indication of health and intelligence.

Their **hair** is light and sometimes curly, with red and golden highlights.

Their **faces** are also triangular, wide at the base and becoming pointed toward the forehead.

Their **facial complexion** is reddish and their skin taut. The skin of their faces is dry, and even their ears, nostrils and eyes appear dry. Their lips are especially dry, and the lack of moisture makes them look rather wrinkled. Their cheekbones protrude, and their ears look like triangles with a rounded base and a protruding apex. Most fire people have open earlobes, and the hollow in the ears hints at openness and an excellent grasp of things.

Their **eyes** are bright and full of vitality, and their eyebrows curve upward; the hair of their eyebrows is a bit springy, especially when they get older.

Their **noses** are pointed, and their cheekbones protrude. Their chins and jawbones are also pointed, and their teeth seem to protrude, too.

Their **skin** radiates warmth and proximity, and they tend to perspire a bit.

Their **voices** are generally hoarse. They speak quickly and jerkily, mainly in order to attract attention.

Their **movements** are quick and sometimes particularly sharp. Fire people are very alert and tend to react speedily.

Their **arms** are muscular and their shoulders bulge.

Their **hands** are long and thin, as are their fingers. Their finger joints bulge, and their palms are generally reddish and liberally lined. Their hands are strong and warm, and as a result, they radiate power when they clap.

Their **legs** are long and flexible, with protruding knees and ankles. Their **feet** are long, thin and bumpy, with protruding bones.

Fire people always look youthful, and are usually thought to be younger than they are. They are vivacious and are extremely active. Standing still is hard for them. They prefer moving to standing, and standing to sitting. Their preferred position is standing with their legs slightly apart, as if in preparation for movement. They are restless, and cannot sit comfortably, because even then they are in a state of readiness for any eventuality.

Their hyperactivity stems mainly from the high rate of metabolism in their bodies. They burn up an enormous amount of energy because of their very active lifestyle, and as a result, they do not gain weight; they always look thin and trim.

Fire people's personality

Let's start with the exceptions: Fat fire people are considered losers. Fire people with plump hands or feet are considered exceptions to their group, unless they have passed their thirties, because by then they have lived a significant part of their lives, and are considered stable and comfortable. Because of the large amount of energy they store, they are excellent at sports, and their physical strength allows them to indulge in activities that are fraught with danger.

Typical illnesses that afflict fire people are fevers, coughs, or depressions, and sometimes accidents resulting from the great number of risks they take.

Fire people's personality is determined by the amount of energy stored in them, and for this reason, these people seek adventures, which help release the enormous store of energy that makes them restless and causes them to seek thrills.

Their inclination to be in perpetual motion leads them to have interesting and intriguing encounters with people and places, and for that reason, their life experience is constantly renewing itself.

Fire people have broad horizons, and because of the rich store of information they have acquired as a result of their quest for adventure, they attract crowds of listeners who admire the extent of their knowledge. Their powers of expression are sophisticated and varied, and their ability to "plug into" any subject almost always places them at the center of any conversation.

It must be pointed out, however, that their great knowledge comes at the expense of profundity; fire people tend to be a bit superficial, as they do not delve into any topic in depth.

Fire people prefer simple, casual clothes to tailored outfits, and usually in shades of red.

They generally prefer loud music, ready-made food, or food that is easily prepared, and noisy, crowded parties. They do not require many hours of sleep, because their thirst for action does not let up for a moment. They are intolerant toward people around them, do not permit others to express themselves, and want to have their say and exert an influence rather than take things in and follow instructions. They cannot understand other people's lack of punctuality, but are themselves not always able to do what they demand of others, which means that they too tend not to be punctual. Since they do not remain angry for long, they expect others to do likewise. Their moods fluctuate quickly, so their anger is short-lived.

Their enormous energy compels them to seek action constantly. They do not enjoy watching others operating, as they are driven by the urge to participate actively in whatever comes along.

Their burning enthusiasm is liable to draw them into dangerous games, gambling, or strange, faraway treks, which take them away from their homes, abandoning those closest to them without a pang of conscience.

Since they are erratic by nature, and not establishment-oriented, their relationships are generally only temporary. They are quite capable of breaking off a love affair abruptly, without considering either the consequences or the pain that the break-up might cause their partner. Their endless eagerness to seek new adventures supersedes love or even parent-children relationships.

Fire people should not find a mate of the same element, since the resulting surfeit of energy will not have a positive effect on them.

Relationships with metal or earth people are sometimes futile, since the combination of these elements will not enable such relationships to develop easily, and the links between them will not thrive. Similarly, they should not develop relationships with water people, because water inhibits fire, and professional or personal relationships will meet with failure.

A combination of fire and wood people enhances the fire people's qualities, since fire is helped by wood, and the combination of the types only succeeds when they can help each other or be helped by each other. When they belong to the same type, or inhibit or are inhibited by another type, the relationship will not work, as conflicts and problems are liable to jeopardize it - or even the partners themselves. This is true for relationships between partners of different sexes or of the same sex.

Fire people are galvanized to action by the energy stored in them. This accounts for their burning desire for success and fame; they want the things they do to be seen, and this motivates them to do more and more.

Because fire people are dynamic and energetic, they are involved in sports and the military (especially when there is action), in advertising, marketing, and journalism, and in professions like fire-fighting and law-enforcement. They can be found on the stage, where they can impress people with their performance, such as in the circus or performing various kinds of stunts.

All of these professions entail a spirit of adventure and the quest for novelty - the more perilous, the better!

However, fire people do not usually remain in any profession for any length of time, and are constantly on the lookout for fresh thrills and challenges. They only start to moderate their behavior when they reach maturity, that is, after the age of 30, an age at which they have already achieved success, and are satiated.

Fire people can be divided into two types:

The first type is stronger and self-motivated, does not give a damn, and ignores consequences.

The second type is more controlled and beneficial, and more considerate of others; their enthusiasm is of longer duration, and they are less ostentatious.

If we were to compare the two types to flames, the first type is like a conflagration that consumes everything in its path, while the second type is like a fire in a fireplace, a warming, pleasant, relaxing and soothing fire which burns slowly and consistently.

As has been mentioned before, "pure" fire people (with no other elements) are rare. Most fire people have characteristics of other elements, and the extent of these additional characteristics determines their individual destinies as well as the things that differentiate them from one another.

The combination of fire and wood

Since fire, which is red, is helped by wood, which is green, their combination results in people with olive complexions, heavier bone structure, and slightly diamond-shaped faces and bodies. The influence of the energy stored in them is toned down, and they possess profundity of thought and intellect. Social consciousness also comes to the fore, as does an affinity for the sciences.

A certain mildness can be discerned in them, as well as stability in relationships or in their jobs. For this reason, their success derives more from the realms of the intellect than from adventurous pursuits.

The combination of fire and water

Since water inhibits fire, the combination of the fire type with the water type is the worst from fire's point of view. The body of the resulting combination is fatter, and since the basic physical build of the fire type is slim and muscular, the "combined" type is liable to develop a tendency to eat and drink excessively.

The combination of fire and water is liable to produce a lazy person, whose stored energy is muted to the point of a loss of interest in life. In fact, all the aspects of his life are inhibited.

The combination of fire and metal

Since fire inhibits metal, the product of this combination is unable to enjoy metal's advantages. The person's complexion is pale, with a tendency to gray, and his physical build is thin. The ambitions and excessive energy that characterize fire people are tempered, as is the curiosity to see, discover, and innovate. This combination results in a person who is satisfied with his achievements, and is not seduced by the fame that comes in the wake of new discoveries. He tends to preserve the status quo rather than seek to increase his knowledge and success.

The combination of fire and earth

Fire helps earth, so earth people are the ones who benefit from this combination. In contrast, fire's action and its dynamic and energetic properties diminish somewhat. In addition, fire people who also have earth characteristics are influenced by the solid physical build of earth types. Their complexion is yellow brown, and the earth influence tones down their energy. Their gait is slower, as are their thought processes, and their ambitiousness is curbed. Their adventurous urge wanes, and their aspirations to fame, which are characteristic of fire people, do not come to the fore.

Wood Types

General remarks

There are two types of wood people.

The first type is tall and bony, resembling a tree with broad branches. Wood people of the first type are intellectual, serious and composed.

The second type is shorter, narrower and - especially - more delicate. Wood people of the second type are rather na(ve, romantic, and a bit superficial.

Both men and women belong to the two wood types, and members of both sexes and types all stand to be successful in their professions, as well as famous and prosperous, whether in the sciences or in the arts. Since they are ruled by Jupiter, which is characterized by growth and expansion, wood people achieve success as a result of academic studies, as the wisdom of this type paves the way for intellectual success.

Physical build: Wood people of the first type are characterized by a fleshy body, covering heavy, protruding (but weak) bones, and muscles that seem insufficiently developed. Wood people of the second type have lighter bones that seem to be concealed by solid flesh.

In both types of wood people, the upper part of the body is longer than the lower part. They have long necks and elongated heads. Their shoulders are broad, creating the shape of an inverted triangle descending toward narrow hips.

Their **heads** are shaped like an inverted triangle, broad at the top, with the crown pointing downward. The upper sides of the head protrude, but become flat further down.

Their **faces**, like their heads, are also shaped like an inverted triangle, with a broad forehead which narrows down to a pointed chin.

Their **facial complexion** is olive - a kind of grayish green - and they often have lines on their foreheads from an early age.

Their **noses** are long and thin.

Their **eyes** are clear and wise, with eyebrows that look as if they have been pencilled on.

Their **ears** are well-shaped, also resembling inverted triangles, and their texture is delicate. It should be noted that the structure of wood people's ears can be an indication of their success in life. The shapelier the ears, the more successful their owner's life.

Their **cheekbones** protrude, but are far from the center of the face.

Their **hair** is of good quality, which explains why wood people like to let it grow. It adds charm to the overall look of their faces.

Their **arms** are long, as are their elbows and the root of their palms.

Their **hands** are long and flat, with tapering **fingers**. Their finger joints bulge. Their palms are solid and usually pale in color, and their handshake is soft and cool, but not weak.

Their **legs** are long and bony, with heavy joints. They have long **feet and toes**. Wood people generally stand with their feet together, and they prefer standing to sitting. It is also typical for them to lean their shoulder against a wall.

The **skin of their bodies** is solid and resembles the bark of a tree. Their movements are energetic, and their speech is sweeping and fluent.

Their **voices** are clear and low, without much inflection.

Their **physical movement** is a bit slack, but their carriage is erect, and they hold their heads up high.

They dress simply. They do not like casual clothing, and prefer light colors to bright, bold ones. They do not follow the dictates of fashion seriously, but choose their clothes carefully, paying attention to good quality.

When they are young, they look older than they actually are, but as they reach maturity, they look their age.

Wood people's personality

They are long-lived, but physical strength does not influence their lives. Conversely, their intellectual prowess and their mental capacities are intact even when their bodies age.

Wood people of the second type do not have a tendency to put on weight (once they reach maturity, their weight basically stabilizes), and even in old age, their bodies are relatively thin.

The fact that they are intellectual people means that they make tremendous cerebral efforts, so that the disorders from which they suffer are mainly nervous tension, anxiety, and the side effects of insomnia and agitation.

Wood people of the first type tend to put on weight as they get older, mainly in the upper part of their bodies. Their legs remain thin.

Since wood people are spaced-out types, their movements are slow and relaxed, and the serenity they enjoy is ongoing, not sporadic and erratic, but gentle and refined. They demonstrate a certain slowness; although they are not athletic types, their bodies are not flabby, and they are fairly well built.

As we said before, since wood people are fundamentally

spaced-out, they are generally dreamy people who tend to go off by themselves and drift off into dreams or ideas. They revel in the company of intellectuals with whom they can exchange ideas, and it is to these people that they will disclose their scientific and humanistic ideas. They do not see the point of idle gossip, so their circle of friends is limited, consisting of thinking people with whom they can share topics of interest.

It is par for the course that wood people require space. They prefer to live in rustic villages, in big houses with picturesque views, where their thoughts are granted the ideal conditions to germinate. They love taking walks, deep in thought, and the tranquil village atmosphere provides them with satisfaction and the possibility of dealing with their own affairs without being disturbed.

Although they can walk great distances, they are not sporty types. If they are asked to participate in a sports contest, they prefer contests that require thought and personal competition.

Their aspiration to win spurs them on, even though they are not competitive by nature.

In spite of their penchant for open spaces, they need a hiding-place in which they can take refuge with their thoughts, inventions and studies. There they feel safe and able to give free rein to their intellectual ability.

Because of their basic tendency to attribute supreme importance to the intellect, wood people usually fall in love with people whom they consider intellectually suitable before trying out the physical side. Only after intellectual compatibility has been established can wood people let go and enjoy sexual relations. When they have created a suitable relationship, wood people are usually very romantic and loving. Their fidelity to their partners is deep and long-lasting.

Wood people's luck is wisdom, which they accumulate over the course of many years, and this is why their fields of interest lie in intellectual professions.

Wood people of the first type excel in the sciences, law, engineering, social sciences, and so on.

Wood people of the second type find their niche in the arts, in research, in discoveries, and so on.

In general, both types of wood people avoid the limelight. For the most part, they are the planning, thinking, checking, and strategic brain behind the scene, or the factor which dictates the ideals and the moral standards (while fire people tend to be the movers and shakers of the project). A successful political party, for example, will select a fire person to be its prospective leader, while wood people will be the ones who dictate party policy.

A combination of wood and wood is not recommended either for personal or professional relationships, since these two spaced-out types do not have a sufficiently solid basis. They are not sufficiently aware of the demands of daily life, which are mainly realistic and consist principally of coping on a day-to-day basis with existential problems such as employment, income, competition, and so on.

The combination of wood people with characteristics of other elements is highly acceptable, occasionally creating sub-characteristics which also become accepted standards.

The combination of wood and water

The most suitable combination for wood people is with water. Water helps wood, providing it with the material things necessary for daily life, as well as the economic successes that derive from water people's money-making abilities. For this reason, water people compensate for what wood people lack by easing the difficulties of earning a living.

Since water helps wood, the combination produces dark-skinned types who tend to put on weight, and for this reason, their bones protrude less, and their faces are slightly round.

The combination somewhat enhances wood people's tendency toward material achievements and fair remuneration for their tireless efforts in the intellectual fields in which they work.

The combination of wood and metal

The combination of wood and metal, which is solid and symbolizes a certain alienation, is not successful from the developmental point of view. The element of metal inhibits wood, and is liable to curtail the intellectual aspirations of wood.

As metal inhibits wood, the combination of the characteristics of metal and wood makes the complexion pale, balances the physical build, and causes the skin to be smoother - resulting in the wood person of the first type, who is stronger physically and interested in material achievements, and not just in developing the intellect, while the wood person of the second type is weaker physically and rather superficial mentally.

The combination of wood and fire

The combination of wood and fire is more beneficial for fire people than for wood people, since wood helps fire. Thus, in the combination with fire, wood's advantages are tempered, and its intellectual abilities do not come to the fore.

As wood helps fire, the combination of their characteristics creates a more active and creative type with a diamond-shaped face and a pinkish complexion.

The combination of wood and earth

The combination of wood and earth is beneficial to wood. Although wood inhibits earth, and is therefore the dominant one of the pair, earth, which requires real security, jeopardizes wood's intellectual aspirations, and in this way, the very factor that determines wood's personality is harmed.

Since wood inhibits earth, the combination of the elements of wood and earth creates a dark-skinned, solidly built type, rather clumsy in its thought processes, less idealistic, and a bit more individualistic. This type is less nervous, less enthusiastic, and less excitable.

Metal Types

General remarks

Generally speaking, metal people are of average height. They have resilient skin which covers healthy bones, and a well-proportioned body. Their forte is mainly in management, and they reach the peaks of success when they are mature. They do not have financial problems, and for this reason rank among the elite of society. Because they are ruled by the planet Venus, they are blessed with talents; for this reason, the path to success is open to them.

Since they belong to the element of metal, which is a solid element, they are characterized by smoothness, elegance, majestic movements and a grace which inspires respect.

Physical build: Metal people's physical build is

average, but proportionate. Their bones are solid, and their flesh and skin are healthy. Their muscles are smooth, and radiate determination. Metal people are never too tall or too short.

The proportions between their body parts are amazingly correct. What makes this type special is their rectangular appearance. Both their heads and their backs are rectangular.

Their **heads** are rectangular, but the upper part is rounded.

Their **foreheads** are smooth and broad.

Their **cheeks** are round, but a bit square at the sides.

Their **noses** are straight.

Their **mouths** are wide, slightly square, and seem to be carefully drawn.

Their **ears** are shapely, with long lobes. They are lighter in color than the rest of the face.

Their **facial complexion** is ivory, and their skin is delicate and fresh.

Their **hair** is lush, smooth and shiny, usually straight and light-colored. Old men's hair is light.

Their **eyes** are big, shiny, and dark.

Their **eyebrows** are long and arched.

Every **facial feature** fits harmoniously into the whole. No feature is disproportionate or spoils the general appearance.

Their **shoulders** are straight.

Their **arms** are rounded and shapely, with smooth elbows and palms.

Their **hands and fingers** are soft and smooth, with narrow finger joints. They have oval fingernails. Their handshake is strong and cordial, and the color of their wrists is pinkish.

Their **hips** are elegantly shaped.

Their **lower limbs** consist of medium-sized thighs and narrow, smooth legs.

Metal women's **breasts** are rounded, full and firm. The men have little hair on their chests.

Their **skin** is soft and shiny, with wonderful coloring.

Their **bodies** are flexible, and their movements are refined and controlled.

Their **voices** are pleasant, creating an atmosphere of intimacy, and they speak clearly and fluently.

Metal people's personality

Metal people's temperament is characterized by great amiability. This can be seen in their delicate walk, their pleasant tone of voice, and in their emotional qualities. These are people who are sure of themselves, whose nature and deeds are controlled by conscious self-criticism. They are calm people, whose walk is sure, upright and rhythmic. They never hurry, nor are they slow. Everything is measured and controlled.

Another indication of their self-control is their insistence on correct nutrition; they do not have a tendency to gain weight. They are fortunate in that even if they are slightly overweight, the excess weight is distributed evenly and proportionately over their bodies, and does not distort their external appearance.

They maintain a balanced diet, but this does not deter them from enjoying fine food that is esthetically served. They never eat or drink excessively - in fact, they do not indulge much in alcohol, and most of them do not smoke.

It is only natural that their youthful and well-preserved appearance does not age rapidly. When they are mature, they look younger than their years, with well-groomed faces and bodies.

By being so self-controlled, they maintain their good health, and are not prone to disease. If they contract a disease, it is generally some kind of respiratory disorder.

Metal people generally do not have many children; in fact, quite a few of them adopt children, or are themselves adopted.

Metal people's natures are refined, and for this reason they are sociable types, who are also very diplomatic and confident. They are popular, and are adept at choosing a social milieu in which they feel comfortable.

They are successful, and know how to enjoy their success. They are involved in whatever is going on around them, but also belong to the big, wide world - and this makes them interesting.

They are knowledgeable about a broad range of subjects, and are up to date with everything that is going on in the world.

They love sports, and enjoy watching sports events. They are art aficionados who not only frequent exhibitions, but often sponsor various types of exhibitions. Despite the fact that they love art and beauty and enjoy elegant surroundings, they are never ostentatious. They never flaunt their wealth or their knowledge, either.

Since they are easy-going and radiate serenity and reliability, they are often invited to social events. People seek to consult with them because their opinion is mature and respected.

They love traveling, and know how to enjoy the good things of life. It seems that they are always in the right place at the right time.

In keeping with their character, their style of dress is solid, elegant and tailored, never ostentatious or fussy. Their clothes are always of the highest quality.

They like good cars, unusual jewelry, fine restaurants, and original works of art.

Since they tend to belong to high society, they are a bit egoistic, but they never neglect their fellow man. They participate extensively in community activities, and can often be seen as donors at charity events.

Their love lives are rather low-key, and they rarely indulge in sexual adventures. Although they respond to love, they hardly ever initiate romantic or sexual relationships. When they do get involved, they are very controlled, and normally do not get swept away by passion.

Because of their basic penchant for status, they tend to select their marriage partners in a calculated way from within their social class. For them, marriage, which occurs once in a lifetime, has a status value; therefore, the appropriate mate must be selected. If they do happen to indulge in a passing affair, their partner will invariably come from a lower social class.

Metal people are very successful in the management field, and excel in positions such as company managers and senior government officials. However, their artistic tendencies place them equally high in the realms of the theater, fashion, media, and so on.

Because of their easy-going character, their broad knowledge, and the serenity they radiate, metal people's greatest success is in the entrepreneurial field. Their good ideas, their superb management skills and methods of utilizing people efficiently help them in every enterprise. Even in enterprises where they are not in charge, they will make their way to the top and take their place among the leaders of the project.

Because of the type of professions they choose, their incomes are generally high, as is their standard of living. However, their success comes slowly, after years of hard work.

There are two types of metal people:

The first type is called the iron type. This is the type which is cast metal, strong and impressive, that can conduct serious entrepreneurial deals. This type includes entrepreneurs, diplomats, judges, senior government officials, and so on.

The second type is more refined, like a piece of finely worked gold in which a precious jewel is set. This type has a penchant for art, opera, and music. It includes actors, advertising executives, artists, architects, and so on.

If we compare the two types, the first runs the election campaign, while the second chooses the slogans for the candidates.

Metal in and of itself is an extremely successful element, but metal people also have and combine with other elements.

It is possible to find "pure" metal types with no other elements in them, but this is rarer than "pure" earth or "pure" water, and much rarer than "pure" fire.

The combination of metal and earth

Since metal is helped by earth, this combination is beneficial to metal people. Earth provides an added value of security, permitting metal people to take risks in material realms in which they do not normally dabble. Since earth helps metal, metal benefits.

The influence of earth creates a more solid person, with strong muscles, a yellowish-brown complexion, and a great capacity for hard work. This person is tuned into security consciousness, but this comes at the expense of some of his personal charm.

The combination of metal and water

Metal helps water, and this cooperation is beneficial for water people's economic situation.

The influence of water is liable to create in metal a tendency toward gaining weight, as well as toward "making money" - that is, a materialistic intrusion into the influences that direct his path in life, and this is the same with the product of this combination.

The combination of metal and fire

The combination of metal and fire is not recommended for metal, since fire melts metal. In more concrete terms, it is clear that the dynamic and adventurous fire person disrupts the serenity and stability of the metal person, undermines his confidence, and damages the status that forms the basis of his equilibrium.

Metal in combination with fire is particularly problematic. As fire inhibits metal, harming metal's properties in consequence, the product of this combination has a pale face, an intolerant disposition, and an irresponsible nature.

The combination of metal and wood

Metal inhibits wood, so that wood suffers from this combination. However, metal is also liable to be influenced by wood's tendency to be spaced-out and slow, thus undermining metal's stability, which is its dominant characteristic.

Metal in combination with wood creates taller people than the usual metal types, with slightly protruding bones, a more developed intellect, and an olive complexion. This combination is not especially successful, since metal, which inhibits wood, will not be influenced by the combination, whereas wood's skills are rendered more superficial than usual.

Water types

General remarks

Water people are smooth, sharp and extremely diplomatic. Generally speaking, they are happy and economically successful. Their luck is wealth, so it is par for the course for them to deal with money. Their main attribute is flexibility, which explains why their relations with those around them are characterized by friendship and calmness. They know how to fit into any social milieu and how to charm everyone.

Their flexibility allows them a lot of room for maneuver in relationships, and they take advantage of their talents to profit from these connections - even to the point of exploiting others so as to fulfill their own personal needs.

Water people have a flair for making friends with the "right people," especially with financiers, and because of their penchant for money, they generally profit from these connections. As a result of their wealth, they lead a luxurious life, traveling extensively, dining in the finest restaurants, and enjoying good domestic lives. They often marry wealthy people, thereby increasing their wealth.

Physical build: The shape of water is round, and water people are round. Their bodies are slightly rounded, their backs are round and protruding, as are their shoulders, hips and thighs. They are fleshy people, but not too overweight. Their bones do not protrude, and they are flexible and nimble. As most water people have short legs, they are short in stature.

Their **heads** are round.

Their **faces** are round and fleshy, and their facial bones do not protrude.

Their **mouths** are wide, dark red, give an impression of moistness, and are generally slightly open.

Their **eyes** are moist, shiny and dark, radiating warmth. Sometimes they droop slightly at their outer edge, but generally they are round, wide-open and protruding.

Their **eyebrows** are dark and arched.

Their **forehead** is rounded, high and unlined.

Their **ears**, which lie close to their heads, are big, round, thick, and pinkish in color. Their earlobes are solid.

Their **noses** are round, sometimes big with a pointed tip.

Their **hair** is dark, thick and straight. The men's beards are dense and dark.

Their **complexion** is dark and their **skin** is fresh.

Their **necks** are round and plump.

Their **backs** are round and long in proportion to their bodies.

Their **shoulders** are round and plump.

Water women's **breasts** are round and full.

Their **hands** are smooth and plump, and their handshake is weak. Their **palms** are generally cool, pale and moist. Their **fingers** are short, smooth, without bulging joints or visible veins.

Their **legs** are also round.

Their **voices** are resonant, clear, and bell-like, and because of this, water people often choose singing as a profession.

Their movements are agile, and they walk loosely.

Because water people are ruled by Star (Mercury) whose characteristic color is black, their skin is dark, and their complexion is excellent - smooth and unwrinkled. Water people often have marks and beauty spots on their skin, which is very moist. Since their temperament is flexible, their walk is also nimble; they do not sway, despite the fact that they are naturally plump. They have a rolling gait - a result of the influence of the circle, which is their basic physical shape.

Despite their agility, water people are not athletic, nor are they particularly active physically. They prefer sitting to standing - but they like lying down most of all. They love dancing, and if they had more of an affinity for movement, they would certainly be good swimmers. They like to sit with friends and enjoy their company and conversation, which does not demand much physical movement, but is very congenial.

As we mentioned before, water people have a tendency to put on weight, and generally speaking, diets are not very effective. They love eating fine food, and their sweet tooth is well known. Since they are not given to much physical activity, their tendency to gain weight prevails. When they put on weight, it affects their entire bodies, especially the region of their midriffs and their limbs. For this reason, water people tend to attribute a great deal of significance to their external appearance - their attire, their make-up and their hairstyle - in order to camouflage their excess fat.

As they are water people, the diseases to which they are prone also reflect a lack of fluids, such as dehydration or difficulties with urination. When they catch cold, it is characterized by a runny nose and streaming eyes; they are also prone to excessive perspiration.

Water people's personality

Water people are by nature sentimental, flexible, adaptable - which means that they are prepared to fit in with the people around them - and opportunistic; they make an effort to enjoy every kind of social milieu.

They radiate serenity and warmth, and are sociable types who inspire trust. People around them rely on them. Not only are they are considered to be discreet, but people see them as suitable shoulders to cry on. Having said this, they are characterized by hot-bloodedness, and are easily aroused by stimuli and passion, especially in sexual relations, where they aim to give more satisfaction than they themselves experience.

Water people's greatest skill lies in making money. For them, money is meant to be used for creating a good life, and for this reason, they enjoy it. While they love the good life, fine food, excellent shows, the joys of travel or of entertainment, they also use money to impress those around them.

In relations between the sexes, their flexibility is again evident in the fact that they do not force their opinions on their partners - neither will they allow themselves to be dominated. They are naturally family-oriented, and their marriages are stable.

They are warm, romantic lovers, whose company is pleasant and entertaining. The men are attentive to their mates, and ply them with gifts, and the women are sensual and seductive. Both men and women enjoy giving their partners love, and they adapt to them easily. Their sexual arousal is quick, but sometimes disappointing.

Since water people's luck is wealth, their main field of interest is money - banking, commerce, or any kind of enterprise. Water people know how to make money and are good at it, and they love the good life that money can bring. They are successful, and tend to marry rich people, thus increasing their wealth.

There are two types of water people:

The first type is aggressive, domineering, and tycoon-like.

The second type is quieter, and accumulates his/her fortune slowly but surely.

If we compare both types to water, the first is a torrent, while the second can be characterized by small waves which are pleasant to wade in.

Since water people's basic characteristic is flexibility, exploiting it allows for maneuvers that result in acquiring wealth in dynamic situations, as well as adapting to whatever is going on around them, all the while exploiting their talent for conducting negotiations. This ultimately leads to the greatest profitability.

While it is true that they are not too keen on physical labor, and generally leave it to others, they make their fortunes in financial matters, in bargaining and in conducting negotiations.

The combination of water and metal

The best partner for water is metal, as water is helped by metal. This combination enhances water people's economic status, and adds an element of elegance and refinement to their lives, possibly even at the expense of their tremendous economic status.

When water people have some characteristics of metal, their complexion is pale, their skin texture is firmer, and their proportions are correct.

The combination of water and earth

Water's worst combination is with earth, since earth inhibits water, decreases its flexibility, and jeopardizes water people's excellent relations with others around them. Earth's influence on water leads to a more materialistic person, a less adaptable one - something that will ultimately harm water's talent for succeeding in business.

The combination of earth and water creates a person whose skin is dark and rough, and whose muscles and bones are tough.

The combination of water and wood

The combination of water and wood is beneficial for wood, since water helps wood, but the water person will develop worries about money that are mainly unjustified. On the other hand, the influence of wood's wisdom will come to the fore, and the person will have intellectual tendencies, but this will come at the expense of a certain degree of financial prosperity. The person will be olive-complexioned, taller, and heavier-boned.

The combination of water and fire

Waters inhibits fire, but even if the combination is more detrimental to fire, water will also not exactly benefit from it. Fire diminishes water's characteristic flexibility somewhat, causing the person to be rather a risk-taker, a bit quicker in his/her decisions, and less calculating, resulting in incorrect decision-making in business and money matters as well.

Earth Types

General remarks

Earth types have a square build, strong bodies, and wise and open minds. Active, healthy, physically fit people, their greatest success lies in the fields of industry, business, agriculture and commerce.

They are not hasty, and "foresight" is their middle name. They operate by devising a plan of action upon which to build their future.

Earth people's **physical build** is square and solid with strong bones, thick thighs and a powerful back. Their torsos are muscular and athletic, and are longer in proportion to their upper and lower limbs.

Their **heads** are square, flat on top, and are supported by short, muscular necks.

Their **hair** is coarse, usually curly and brown or chestnut-colored. The men have a full, heavy beard.

Their **foreheads** are square and smooth.

Their **eyes** are also square in shape, and they radiate energy and action.

Their **faces** are square, with thick, solid skin. Their bones do not protrude, and even their cheekbones are hardly visible because they are so flat.

Their **noses** are big and protruding.

Their **ears** are thick and quite big. Their earlobes are round and well shaped.

Their **jaws** are also square and solid.

Their **mouths** are big, broad, and square.

The **bones** of their bodies are heavy and mainly flat, but do not protrude. Their powerful muscles bulge.

Their **arms** are solid and muscular.

Their **hands** are heavy and muscular, square and stubby.

Their **fingers** are short, and their handshake is firm.

Their **wrists**, which are brown and yellowish, are strong and warm.

The **women's breasts** are large and full, while the **men's chests** are solid and muscular.

Their muscular **legs** are relatively short and the bones do not protrude.

Their **skin** is thick and dark-colored. A suntan makes their skin beautiful, healthy, and bronze.

Their **voices** are deep, and their speech is clear and ringing, almost monotonous.

Their **posture** is upright, and their powerful build radiates strength and health.

Earth people's personality

Earth people are quiet by nature. Although they tend to show off their strength, they are not especially active. They prefer standing to walking, but sitting is their favorite position. They are economical, slow and quiet in their movements. However, this does not mean that they are timid. This type has presence, both internal and external.

The earth type is suited more to hard work than to athletic activities. Earth people persevere in their work, and prefer to be static and stable, both in their choice of profession and in the various aspects of their lives. They are independent, and shoulder responsibility both at work and in their personal lives; they expect others to do likewise. Nevertheless, they are prepared to come to other people's aid if necessary, as they are basically good, understanding, and considerate people.

Earth people are calm, trustworthy, clever, and successful, who by nature prefer security to any kind of risk. This means that they are not too open to trying new things. For this reason, their social circle is fairly limited, but is compatible with their nature.

Because of their desire for security in their lives, they are drawn to occupations involving money and industry. Earth people work hard throughout their lives in order to attain the economic stability that brings the coveted security.

Generally speaking, they begin their careers at the bottom of the ladder, and advance to the most senior positions. On their way up, they accumulate money and possessions - although money is not their primary objective, but rather a means to attain security, which is what they are really aiming for.

They are conservative by nature, and are not big risk-takers; they certainly do not gamble if their future is at stake. Earth people can be found in many professions, such as industry, construction, real-estate, commerce, and so on.

There are two types of earth people: The first type is very aggressive and domineering. People of this type are not flexible, and their decisions are immutable. This type can be found mainly in construction and branches of heavy industry.

The second type is more delicate, earth-oriented and deep-rooted. These people are efficient, productive, and extremely serious. They can be found in agriculture, construction, and commerce.

Both earth types are hardworking and successful, and are prepared to invest a lot of energy and strength in order to succeed. They generally head companies because of their ability to shoulder responsibility and accomplish objectives in the best possible manner, and particularly because of their leadership abilities.

By the age of approximately forty, they achieve their aims, but continue to work energetically for many years. They never throw in the towel, never give up or retire, and unless old age ultimately prevails, they just keep on going.

Other people are fond of earth people because they are better listeners than they are talkers; however, when they have to express an opinion, they do so succinctly and with extreme precision.

They take life very seriously, and attribute importance - which is sometimes exaggerated - to the values which they hold dear, such as money and politics.

As we mentioned before, the accumulation of wealth and possessions is not the principal objective of earth people. What they desire most is security, and money is the means to attain it.

For this reason, money is not meant for speculative purposes such as gambling, nor is it to be used ostentatiously or for purposes of influence. A fat bank balance ensures future security more than a trip around the world, which uses up one's resources.

In contrast to their serious image when it comes to earth-shattering matters, they enjoy good entertainment, and laugh heartily at a good joke; this acts as a safety-valve against unnecessary thoughts.

Women of the earth type seek security in their domestic lives and in raising their children more than in the choice of a professional career.

Earth people can enjoy athletic activities which demand

the use of their muscles rather than movement. As they age, there is a decrease in their physical activity.

As their name indicates, earth people love being in the heart of nature, in a green and blooming environment. Their deep-rootedness comes to the fore in their choice of hobbies such as gardening or raising pets. This is, of course, on condition that they are not removed from their immediate static framework.

Since they are very muscular, they appear heavyset, but this is merely an optical illusion. They look older than they really are, and even when they are young, they look like people who are settled and firmly based in life, although in fact this only happens when they are mature. As they grow older, they appear a bit heavier, even though their body is made up of muscles.

Relations between the sexes are also influenced by the preoccupation with future security.

Earth people tend to establish themselves, live a peaceful life, and raise children. They are practical in their choice of a mate, which is a serious matter to them, and their relationship with their mate is also serious. They have a lot of children, and indulge in sexual relations up to an advanced age.

As we have mentioned before, when combining elements, one should avoid choosing a partner of the same element. However, when choosing mates, earth people sometimes choose other earth people, since they share the objective of attaining security, and this dictates their needs and their way of life. Since they do not have other dominant aspirations which are liable to damage their relationship, this combination is successful, as it leads to a harmonious, unpretentious domestic life which answers the basic needs of the earth.

The combination of earth and fire

When it comes to business, the best combination for earth is with fire, as fire helps earth and gives it movement and color. Fire contributes energy and action to placid earth, and stimulates earth to enjoy adventures and to take an interest in life - or even to take low-level, but tempting, risks.

This combination produces a person with a reddish complexion, a bit less solid as a result of fire's influence, but more flexible and more dynamic.

The combination of earth and metal

Earth helps metal, which means that metal is the main beneficiary in this combination. However, earth enjoys a limited amount of metal's influence, especially in the realm of interest in art and entering fields that require more profound thinking.

The person is more delicate both in his or her characteristics and build, a little more diplomatic, less blunt, and is interested in developing and creating a firm basis for his or her status in society.

People of this combination have lighter, smoother, less coarse and more refined complexions.

The combination of earth and water

Earth inhibits water, so that while there could be a negative influence on water, earth is likely to gain skills in monetary matters which are worth implementing. The person has a greater interest in money - not just in what money can provide, but as an objective per se.

There can also be an emotional influence, and a certain degree of openness can be discerned as a result of the combination.

This combination produces a darker complexion, as well as a tendency to put on weight.

As a result of this combination, the quest for security may be somewhat diminished, and there may even be cases of risk-taking - calculated, generally speaking - but as the earth person is not accustomed to taking risks, there is a fear of failure.

The combination of earth and wood

	Fire	Water	Wood	Metal	Earth
Shape of Face	Triangular	Round	Inverted triangle	Rectangular	Square
Complexion	Ruddy	Dark	Olive	Ivory	Tanned
Skin Type	Dry	Moist	Taut	Fresh	Solid
Hair	Curly	Thick	Straight	Fine	Coarse
Ears	Sharp	Fleshy	Long, thin	Round	Big
Eyes	Sparkling	Lit up	Clear	Light	Wise
Nose	Sharp	Round	Long	Delicate	Big
Build	Bony	Fleshy	Rugged	Shapely	Muscular
Skin	Taut	Loose	Solid	Smooth	Heavy
Physical Build	Slim, muscular	Round	Thin	Well-shaped	Solid
Physical appearance	Alert	Calm	Erect, tall	Complex	Massive
Reaction	Quick	Flowing	Sweeping	Graceful	Slow

Earth is inhibited by wood, and earth people's self-confidence is in danger of being eroded by wood's tendency to "float" and change things, while earth's nature is static, and does not take to changes easily. The person resulting from this combination is rather idealistic, humanistic and intellectual. From the physical point of view, he or she is weaker and taller with a pale or greenish complexion.

The Combination of Types

Pure, unadulterated types - those which do not contain any other elements - are rare. Most people have one basic element, which is generally obvious, seeing that it is dominant in a certain type, but it is combined with the characteristics of other elements, such as hair color, complexion, and so on. Combinations sometimes work to the benefit of the person, but conversely sometimes spoil positive characteristics. The degree of influence depends on which secondary element is in the combination, and the extent of its dominance.

The most notable "combined" types are as follows:

The **fire type** contains a bit of beneficial wood. Wood is an element characterized by wisdom, and therefore it enhances the fire type's intellect, as fire is adventurous and spontaneous rather than intellectual.

On the other hand, fire is inhibited by water, and for this reason, the slim, muscular fire type, under the influence of water, will be shorter, rounder, darker, less spontaneous and less curious about innovations or adventures.

The **wood type** is helped by water, which means that the combination of water and wood will improve the person. The financial ability which characterizes water will improve the economic situation of wood, which is basically a "spaced-out" type whose primary interest does not lie in everyday material matters.

On the other hand, wood is inhibited by metal, so that the combination of metal and wood will be to the detriment of wood's intellectual successes, and will make the person more superficial. However, the first wood type, which is stronger, will suffer less from the combination.

The **water type** is helped by metal, which means that the resulting combination of water and metal will be a person with extensive possessions and a lot of influence. Water is inhibited by earth, so that the combination of water and earth will be less successful and more materialistic.

The **metal type** is helped by earth, which provides him with cool-headedness in business, and as a result, there are especially big economic successes. However, if metal, which is inhibited by fire, is mixed with fire, it becomes restless and impatient, and for this reason metal's success is liable to be diminished, and its great status will be undermined.

The **earth type** is helped by fire, which means that the combination with fire's characteristics contribute energy and activity to earth. However, if earth is combined with wood, its action is inhibited. The earth type, which is quiet by nature, is liable to become apathetic, and lose the feeling of security that characterizes it.

The product that results from these combinations depends on the influence of the extraneous elements. In spite of this, sub-groups of combinations of characteristics can be identified. These characteristics manifest themselves particularly in hair and skin color. In other words, it is easier to discern visible physical attributes than character traits.

The most obvious sub-groups in physical build are the diamond shape, the elliptical shape and the heart shape.

These three types are based on combinations with the wood type, the most widespread type.

The diamond shape - the combination of wood and fire

This combination produces a diamond-shaped face, which is the product of the combination of the two triangles which characterize the archetype both of wood and of fire. The top of the head is pointed, broadening in the region of the cheekbones, and narrowing again in the jaw region.

The body is also tall and diamond-shaped: It is narrow at the shoulders, becoming broader in the thigh region, and narrowing again toward the feet.

This shape is particularly noticeable in career women, but there are also men with this build. People with this build are generally successful, combining the energy and curiosity that they get from fire with the depth and intellectual knowledge that derive from wood.

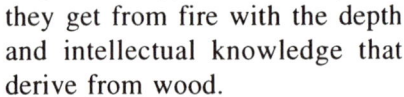

It goes without saying that the combination is slightly detrimental to each characteristic, coming at the expense of absorbing a characteristic from the other element, but in the final analysis, the resulting people are successful, especially in business and enterprises, and this comes to the fore in their thirties or forties. However, their enthusiasm wanes with the onset of old age.

The elliptical shape - the combination of wood and metal

The shape of the face that results from this combination is elliptical - narrow and rounded at the crown, broadening in the region of the ears, and narrowing and rounding again in the neck region. The combination of wood and metal creates an oval chin.

The shape of the body is also elliptical, like an egg, sometimes rounder and broader at the shoulders, becoming narrower and rounded in the thigh region.

Wood's influence makes the person tall and bony, while metal's influence causes the person's body to be proportionate. The person that results from this combination is handsome, so the type is evident among women. For this reason, good-looking women generally work in professions which highlight their beauty, such as modeling, photography, acting, and so on. Men of this combination tend to work in photography.

The economic status of these people is high thanks to metal's influence, but also thanks to wood, which is responsible for the intellectual side and the desire to study and reap profits.

Their success is not long-lived, and as they grow old, it fades as a result of the aging of body and soul, occasionally abandoning the person altogether.

The heart shape - the combination of wood and water

This type is a combination of wood's inverted triangle and water's round shape, creating a heart shape.

The person's head is heart-shaped, with the crown marking the meeting-point of the two halves of the heart, and from there the two half-circles emerge, broadening toward the ear region, and narrowing toward the neck region.

The hair is also heart-shaped; the middle of the forehead marks the meeting-point of the two halves of the heart. The face, too, is heart-shaped, with broad cheekbones which narrow toward the chin.

The body is also heart-shaped, rounded in the region of the shoulders, and narrowing toward the thighs.

The limbs are short, and under water's influence, the person has a tendency to gain weight.

The combined type contains some of wood's characteristic wisdom and water's flexibility. Water promises

success in the social, intellectual and emotional realms, coming as a result of in-depth study more than from economic topics. These people reach the pinnacle of success in their forties. Women have a marked tendency to marry men of status and respectability rather than achieving these things by their own efforts.

Since these people are

sociable and friendly, they are popular with the people around them. They take advantage of their ability to establish good contacts to accumulate power and influence.

The combinations of wood with water, metal, and fire are characterized by temporary success.

Success occurs in their thirties and forties, but is not long-lived.

With old age comes the decline, manifesting itself in weakness, spiritual and physical fatigue, and loss of social influence.

The Various "Animal" Types

Among the types, there is a section in which typical physical builds of men and women are compared to certain animals. In the animal world, the archetype generally comes to the fore in the males, although sometimes it can be discerned in the females. In birds, the archetype mainly comes to the fore in the females.

There are two exceptions: The dragon is always male, and the phoenix is always female.

As is the case with human beings, the unadulterated type is the most successful. The dragon, which is a mystical creature, is certainly an unadulterated type, representing the perfect animal; so the person who has the physical build of an unadulterated type of animal is in fact perfect.

There are five types of animals that are mainly "masculine":

The tiger type

Tiger types are of medium size, with strong and bony bodies. They have big heads, which are broad at the cheekbones, and high foreheads.

Their eyes are big, round and shiny, with lustrous pupils. Their eyebrows are arched, and their ears are small and pointed with slightly protruding tips. Their mouths are big and wide, with thick lips. Their teeth are big and strong, and their upper jaw fits the lower jaw well, so that when they close their mouths, their teeth are a perfect match.

Their muscles are smooth and solid, and their shoulders square and strong.

Their voices are loud, slightly high and strident.

Tiger types are very aggressive, sometimes cruel, and they are generally leaders because of their aggressiveness. Their athletic bodies ensure them great agility, and they have no trouble avoiding pitfalls and perils.

The lion type

Lion types are big and strong, but their bodies are not as strong as the tiger's; because of their slack muscles, they are also less agile.

Their faces are round, becoming somewhat pointed in the region of the lower jaw. Their foreheads are high, and their eyebrows are dense and arched. Their eyes are big, piercing, and frightening, so that their gaze is serious and attests to authority.

Their noses are big and broad at the base, and their nostrils are rounded at the top and slightly flatter at the sides. Their lips are big, protruding and well-shaped.

Their voices are deep and clear.

Lion types have a wide range of possibilities available to

them when choosing a profession. They can succeed in industry as well as in business. They are congenial by nature, and it is pleasant to work and socialize with them, as they are very humane. Despite their serious external appearance, inside they are extremely amiable.

The dragon type

This type is rare - in fact, it hardly exists at all. It is the leader, ruler, and unique type. Dragon types are handsome, with well-shaped bodies. Their heads are medium-sized with curved and shapely foreheads. Their eyes are big and luminous, wide near the nose and gradually narrowing toward the ears. Their eyebrows are arched, and not too thick. Their noses are in the center of their faces, descending in a straight line from the area of the eyes with no gap between them. The tips of their noses are rounded, and the nostrils are round and thin. This kind of nose is successful in other types as well.

Their mouths are wide, with full, ripe, slightly square pink lips which look as if they have been painted on. These lips attest to a compassionate and considerate nature.

Their voices are deep and resonant.

Dragon types are compassionate, generous and warm. They are successful, and accumulate power and property throughout their lives. They exert a great influence on the people around them - usually a good influence. They do favors for others, and are active in charitable organizations; in return, they are given abundant warmth and affection.

The horse type

The bodies of horse types are long and bony, with long limbs long and protruding stomachs. Their heads are slightly elongated, as are their faces. They have high foreheads, large, wide eyes, long noses, and broad mouths. Their ears are long, with pointed earlobes. Horse types speak quickly, and, as a result, indistinctly.

They get on well with those around them, and are well-liked because of their willingness to listen to others.

They are successful, but far from being perfect; that is, they succeed in realizing their aspirations, which are not necessarily material aspirations.

They work hard to accomplish their objectives, often encountering obstacles along the way. They sweat like horses and work hard. They are responsible and serious types who do not necessarily reach the top. However, they realize most of their aspirations, and are satisfied with that. They know how to enjoy their achievements.

The bull type

These types do not look like bulls. They are not necessarily bony or heavy. Most of the time they are of medium build and delicate appearance, with a certain discernible gentleness in their movements.

Their heads are round, with high foreheads, big round eyes, long eyebrows and thick, straight lashes.

Bull types speak slowly, and are dreamy, and not usually realistic. They are creative and talented, but do not come anywhere near realizing their dreams. They are not entrepreneurs, and although they can perform certain tasks skillfully, they cannot initiate long-term operations, nor can they control big enterprises which demand comprehensive, global vision and powerful management.

There are five types of birds that are mainly "feminine":

The crane type

Crane types are tall and thin, with small heads and pointed features. They have narrow foreheads, small eyes, and narrow eyebrows. Their noses are small, their lips are thin and narrow, and their necks are long and slightly wrinkled. They have narrow shoulders, and long, thin arms and legs.

Their voices are high and sharp.

Crane types are liable to appear sickly, and sometimes inspire pity; for this reason, they are not successful, and do not have a lot of luck.

The unadulterated crane types are quick, alert and agile. Their movements are light, and they are successful. They become rich easily, and women of this type either marry wealthy men, or succeed thanks to their own talents.

The dove type

Dove types are of medium build, with a handsome body slightly on the plump side. Their skin is smooth and their eyes are small and shiny. They have round heads, small foreheads and noses, and smooth facial skin. Their lips are rounded and shapely, and their ears are round and close to their heads. Their voices are low and cooing, like a dove's.

Dove types (almost always female) are wives and mothers who worry about their families and take care of them warmly and anxiously. Sometimes the people close to them take far too much advantage of them, and exploit them for their own purposes. Generally speaking, dove types do not challenge authority, and do what is demanded of them. Nevertheless, these types are withdrawn, and internalize their feelings.

Dove types are capable of being very creative, but they do not involve others in their activities, nor do they display their success in public. Their success is manifested in their relationship with their spouses and in the upbringing of their children. They prefer to see their families succeeding, and are satisfied with the security their family members create for them.

The eagle type

The eagle is tall and stooped, with strong, pointed body parts. Eagle types have elongated heads, high necks, long, narrow eyes, and pointed eyebrows. Their lips are narrow, their chins are solid, and their noses are strong, bony, and pointed at the end.

Although esthetic principles cannot be applied to these types, their appearance is impressive, and they have a commanding presence.

Eagle types are brilliant, sharp, outstandingly perceptive, and excellent at implementing things.

These types are quite aware of their appearance, and they have the ability to improve it. After considerable efforts, they can look immeasurably better.

Eagle types know how to act, and, by making an effort, can succeed. They do not give up; they aspire to reach the top, and utilize all their strength to get there.

In general, both females and males of the eagle type are business people who never lose sight of their goal to create a secure future for themselves and to accumulate property and social standing.

The phoenix type

Phoenix types are regal.

Their faces are rectangular, as are their foreheads. Their eyes are slightly slanted, and their eyebrows look as if an artist has painted them. They have straight, upturned noses. Their mouths are round or, occasionally, square.

Their appearance is elegant, and their bodies are proportionate. They have excellent complexions that radiate purity and smoothness.

Their voices are gentle but clear as a bell.

Like the unadulterated dragon in the male, so the unadulterated phoenix in a woman is a manifestation of the perfect type.

The swan type

Swan types are thin, tall, with long swan-like necks, and a more elegant appearance than that of the crane.

Their heads are elongated, with high foreheads, and round, dark eyes. They have straight noses with small nostrils. Their mouths are round, and their lips look as if they have been painted on. Their facial and body skin is smooth and free of blemishes, and the sum total of head and body parts creates a pleasing and handsome appearance.

Swan types (who are almost always female) do not have a flair for making money, but when they have clear dark eyes, their chances of material success are high. If their eyes are not shiny, success will be partial, and they will most probably be lonely in their old age. Moreover, their marriages will not necessarily be successful.

Generally speaking, success is temporary, and will dissipate completely when they reach old age. This is true for the pure swan type as well.

The Role of Cosmic Energies in Shaping the Body

According to ancient Chinese knowledge, two cosmic energies work together to create the life force. The first - the masculine - is called *yang*, and the second - the feminine - is called *yin*.

In the body, the hard bones symbolize the masculine, or yang, while the delicate parts, like the flesh and skin, represent the feminine, the yin. A good body contains both masculine and feminine parts, creating a balance of cosmic energies, which leads to harmony in the body. In other words, a body in which the amount of energy is balanced will be successful from every point of view. For example, a body of this type will not have a tendency to gain weight, while a body that is overweight or underweight indicates a surfeit or lack of yin or yang.

Metal is noteworthy for the balance between the two kinds of energy, which means that the metal type does not gain weight, and his or her body always remains balanced.

The wood and fire types indicate a surplus of masculine energy in the body, which means that they do not tend to gain weight.

Water and earth have a surplus of feminine energy, which means that they tend to put on weight (water has a tendency toward weight gain, while earth has a tendency toward heavy muscles).

There are people whose weight gain is distributed all over their bodies, while others tend to gain weight in particular places. In general, men tend to get a paunch, while women become broad around the thighs. However, four types of weight gain can be characterized in greater detail:

The first type: women and men who gain weight all over their bodies.

The second type: weight gain in the upper part of the body, while the lower part remains the same (characteristic of men).

The third type: heavy thighs and upper bodies (characteristic of women).

The fourth type: weight gain in the lower part of the body, while the upper part remains the same (characteristic of women)*.

The range of cosmic energies extends beyond the simplistic divisions of the human body, reaching the personality and the brain, whose influence dictates the harmony between body and soul.

Since the yin and yang energies are responsible for the life force, they should be examined more closely in order to understand their influence in the desired balance between body and soul.

The masculine yang consists of the solid, bony, active, intellectual skeleton which operates during the day and resembles the sun. It is active and contains the power of work and creativity. It is the yang that paves the person's place and status in life.

The feminine yin is emotional, receptive, softer and darker; it operates at night and resembles the moon. It has a tendency toward cultural activity and social life, and strives toward establishing the family unit.

---

*In order to regulate the body fats so that all body parts are proportionate, it is recommended to take a hot bath and to massage the body, particularly along the meridians and pressure points that are responsible for regulating weight. This increases blood circulation and accelerates metabolism, so that the fats are distributed evenly.

The balance between the two types of energy creates harmony in the human body and in the entire universe.

The yang protects the inner yin organs of the body, but the harmony that is created between the two energies that generate the two different kinds of activities is the harmony that sustains life.

The action of the two energies mentioned above can in fact be found in all realms, which always combine in matching active with passive, and find each other, when the one is more dominant, and the other, which is passive, accepts the dominant one's authority.

The Body's Proportions

The body has three regions which symbolize characteristics according to physical build.

The **first region** is the head, and it is responsible for personality and the potential for achievement. This region should be *one seventh* of the length of the entire body.

The **second region** includes the neck, the shoulders, the arms, and reaches the waist. This region is responsible for physical strength, for profession and for health. This region should be double the head region in length, which means *two sevenths* of the length of the entire body.

The **third region** consists of the part of the body between the waist and the toes. This region is responsible for physical build and intellectual daring. This region should be four times the size of the head region, which means *four sevenths* of the length of the entire body.

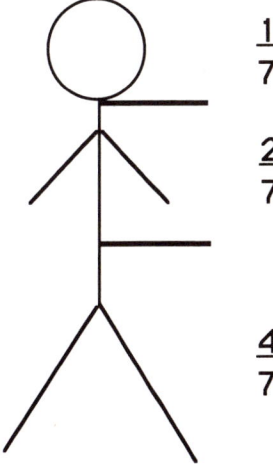

$$\frac{1}{7}$$

$$\frac{2}{7}$$

The ratios between these three regions create types of differing potential.

The three most obvious types appear in the diagrams that follow:

$$\frac{4}{7}$$

First type:

The head region is longer than one seventh, the second region is longer than two sevenths, and the third region is short.

This type is intellectual, a clever person who prefers studying to working, and who is not materialistic.

People of this type tend to engage in writing or teaching, and since they are ambitious and have the power to supervise, they attain senior positions and a high rate of achievement.

The second type:

There is a balance between the regions, that is, one seventh : two sevenths : four sevenths. People of this type are perfect. Their attributes are varied, and they are successful both in intellectual and practical fields, in science, and in financial management. If they engage in the humanities, such as writing or acting, they will display their numerous talents; in fact, these people are successful in everything they do.

The third type:

The head region is shorter than one seventh, the second region is shorter than two sevenths, and the third region is long. These people are particularly physical and their cerebral side is less pronounced. They engage in sport, the military or law-enforcement, and since they are adventurous types, they will change professions a few times during the course of their lives. These people like taking risks, preferring this to building stable lives. Thus, their success depends on their chances of becoming well-known more than on their aspiration to financial stability.

It is likely that the metal type has a balanced build, and belongs to the second type, while the fire type belongs to the third. Wood belongs to both the first and the third, while earth belongs to the first and the second. Water also belongs to the first and third types.

CHAPTER TWO

THE BODY IN DETAIL

According to the ancient Chinese system of reading the body's secrets, each organ is significant in constructing the life of the individual, as well as in his or her choice of a profession, and in forecasting the person's potential and possible achievements.

It must be remembered that according to this system, in spite of the fact that physical build is generally permanent, it can be improved, or even rebuilt, so as to make the most of it. Fats, muscles, voice, and so on, can be "improved," built, or diluted according to what is necessary.

Reading the body in detail

Every part of the body has an ideal size and shape, as determined by the specific function of the part. An individual analysis of each organ enables us to identify its weakness and to improve it according to its role in the body.

The main objective of reading the body is to get to know it, to connect to it, to feel at one with it, until we reach the point where we understand and know the essence of our self, and can also practice and improve the functioning of each organ separately, and of the body as a whole.

The head

The head is the first part of the body, and is responsible for the person's intellectual activity, for his cerebral ambition, and for his ability to attain a high status as a result of his achievements in the various realms of life.

The head's uniqueness results from its location in the upper part of the body, as well as of its being the seat of the brain and the mind. In addition, the head contains the four senses (excluding touch) by means of which we absorb extra-physical influences.

When we examine the head, we examine its shape, the way the shape of the bones reflects the cosmic energies, and the proportions between the parts of the head that are covered with hair - the yin parts - and the exposed parts - the yang parts.

Size

A big head attests to great wisdom, to a high degree of intelligence, and to greater spirituality than intellectuality.

A medium-size head attests to a developed mind, to good physical abilities, and to multifaceted characteristics.

A small head attests more to a tendency toward adventure and experimentation than to intellectual achievements attained by study and research.

The bigger the head, the greater the likelihood of intellectual success, which is expressed in senior positions and high standing, although senior positions can be obtained both in the realms of art and by means of physical daring.

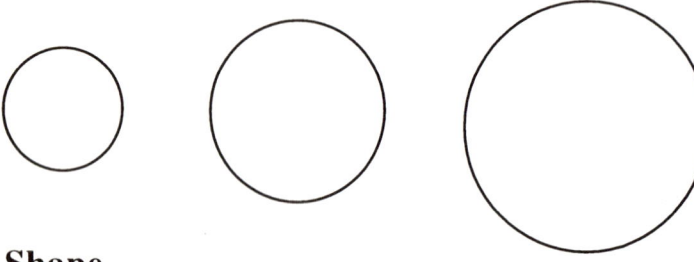

Shape

Heads have the following basic shapes: square, round, rectangular, double triangle, and conical.

A square head is distinguished by its forehead, the upper part of which is straight; from each end, the sides of the face descend vertically, with minor protrusions in the region of the ears, down to the base of the lower jaw, where the chin is almost completely flat.

This kind of head indicates that the person will attain status by means of hard work, perseverance and precise planning.

A round head is exactly that - as round as a ball, and even the ears are close to the head, and do not distort the perfect circle.

This kind of head indicates a person who operates emotionally rather than rationally. This person attains a high status by means of property and tactics and maneuvers that are sometimes accompanied by cunning.

A **rectangular head** is elongated, narrow in the region of the forehead, becoming even narrower in the region of the lower jaw, until it is very short and narrow in the region of the chin. This kind of head indicates a person who attains status by means of cautious and calculated management, and the accumulation of property.

A **double triangle head** is elongated at the sides of the face, becoming narrow in the region of the top of the head, and descending from the region of the lower jaw to the short, flat chin.

This head indicates a person who attains status by means of mental ability, and by engaging in the sciences and in art.

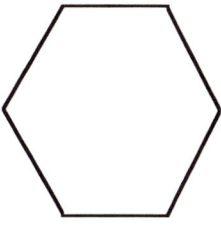

A **conical head** is broader in the region of the top of the head, becoming narrower as it descends to the short, flat chin.

This head indicates a person who establishes his basis in life by means of physical activity or physical talents in fields such as acrobatics or displays of physical virtuosity.

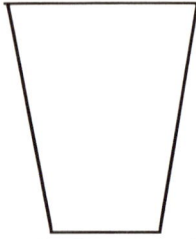

In each shape of head, there are five regions in which protuberances can be found: the nape, the forehead, the crown, and the two sides. The important phenomena that must be examined here, similar to the art of phrenology, are:

If **the nape, the crown, and the forehead protrude**, the person is congenial, organized, positive, honest and reliable. By nature, the person is congenial, has a sense of humor, is generous, and donates money to others. His thought processes are serious and profound, and he is successful. His success lies in business, especially in industry, but also in research and inventing.

If **the nape protrudes and the forehead is broad and flat**, the person is blessed with leadership abilities, is able to manage and supervise other people, and is courageous and creative. The person has a good grasp of things, as well as the ability to stick to a task, and is capable of making the correct decisions by means of serious and profound thought processes. These people succeed in senior positions which demand excellent leadership abilities, the ability to stick to a schedule, and the precise implementation of the task at hand.

If **the nape and the crown protrude, and the forehead is broad (but does not protrude),** the person is especially talented. This is an intellectual who devotes himself to studies or research, and has the soul of an artist. Generally speaking, he is an idealist, and is sometimes a bit spaced out. He attains the most senior positions very easily, and particularly enjoys being involved in science and research, teaching or art.

If **the crown protrudes, but the forehead and nape do not**, the person reaches the peak of his activity in his youth, before the age of 25. Sometimes, the person is restless and unstable, which means that he has to decide on a profession at a young age, worry about establishing himself, and avoid long-term ambitions, as his strength and ability will not endure in the long term. In his youth, he is active, but as he gets older, so his physical and mental strength wane.

If **the head is square with protruding sides**, the person is considered successful, both professionally and materially. This person is hardworking and consistent, loyal to his superiors and to those around him, and tends to spend a lot of time and expend a great deal of energy on his work. His financial situation is very good, and he enjoys good interpersonal relationships. He has a long life-span, during which he gains the sympathy of those around him. Many people admire him and seek his company because of his good name and reliability.

Holding one's head
The way a person holds his head indicates his degree of success in life. The head is an indication of success, and the higher it is held, the greater the achievements, and the higher the status of the person.

A head that is held high is not merely an expression of confidence, but also an indication of the person's path in life, of his career and of his successes.

The face

The face is divided into three regions (sometimes called "stations").

The **first region** extends from the lower edge of the hairline to the center of the eyebrows. It is an indication of character and represents the person's youth up to the age of 30.

The **second region** extends from the center of the eyebrow line to the base of the nose. It is an indication of early middle age, that is, from 30 to 50. This region represents achievements in life.

The **third region** extends from the base of the nose to the base of the chin. This region is an indication of maturity, that is, from the age of 50 onward. It represents longevity.

The characterization of the facial features according to yang and yin:

When the forehead, the cheekbones, the nose and the chin protrude, the person is considered to be fortunate. These features belong to the yang and are called *mountains*.

The mountains should protrude and should be located in the place that is meant for them; this will ensure their owner a fortunate and successful destiny.

The organs that produce moisture, such as the eyes, ears, nostrils and mouth, belong to the yin and are called *rivers*.

The rivers must be clear, clear and moist in order to ensure stability in life.

The ears

The location of the ears is significant in the analysis of the person's future: the location of the upper tip of the ear in relation to the eyebrow is examined.

Ears that are located high up, with their upper tip above the horizontal line of the eyebrow, attest to success that begins in the person's youth.

Ears that are located at an average height, with their upper tip in line with the horizontal line of the eyebrow, attest to economic success in the person's thirties and forties.

Ears that are located low down, with their upper tip lower than the horizontal line of the eyebrow, attest to modest success in the person's later years.

Perfect ears should be large, solid and shapely, and they must be located at an average height. They must be close to the head, but not adjoining it.

The lobe should be long, which is a sign of a long life and great wisdom. If the hollow of the ear is big, it means an excellent ability to grasp and absorb things. Behind the ear, the bone should protrude, as this also attests to longevity.

The color of the ears should be lighter than that of the face.

The forehead

The ideal forehead tends to be square. It attests to good fortune if the bones protrude. A high forehead indicates good ancestry, and if an eldest son is the subject in question, he will be supported by his parents all the way. If the forehead is high, but the subject in question is not the eldest son, the opposite will occur, and his parents will depend on him in their old age.

The eyebrows

Protruding eyebrows are an advantage. They represent fame and glory, and if they are arched, smooth, and shiny as silk, they are an indication of good fortune and glory. There should be a space between them - ideally a space of two finger-widths.

The eyes

The eyes are an indication of wisdom, and when they are full and shiny, they attest to deep understanding and a high degree of intelligence. They should not be too close together, but not too far apart either. The perfect distance between them is the width of one eye.

The cheekbones

This relates to the two cheekbones - the one that connects the bone of the eye to the temple, and the one in the middle of the face with the bumps at the end. They are both indications of strength, and the more they protrude, the greater the power. The cheekbones should not be too close to the nose.

The nose

The nose is an indication of wealth and health in the person's thirties and forties. The more the nose is straight, thin, and protruding, the greater the person's wealth and health.

The jawbone

The jawbone is an indication of status. When it is square, it ensures good status in life.

The chin

The chin is an indication of power. When it is square and protruding, its owner will be powerful even in old age.

The mouth

The mouth is an indication of personality. When it is big and well-shaped, it ensures good fortune.

The teeth

The teeth represent the stomach. The ideal situation is one in which all the teeth are white, straight, average in size, and close together without gaps. When they fulfill these criteria, they indicate intelligence, a good character, a positive personality, and attest to a good life, a warm family unit, and success in business.

The tongue

The tongue represents the heart. Its color should be pinkish, neither too red nor not too pale. A long, curling tongue attests to a very powerful heart and a high level of vitality.

The cleft

The cleft between the nose and the upper lip represents the body's fertility. When it is deep, long, smooth and unwrinkled, it is a sign of success, ensuring sexual prowess even in old age. If it is too light, it attests to a body full of toxins. If it is too dark, it signifies accidents.

Men whose beards grow within the borders of the cleft are fortunate.

The hair

The head in its entirety is considered yang - masculine energy - especially the parts that are not covered with hair. But the hair itself is considered yin - feminine energy - and as such is emotional, maternal, and sensitive.

The hair attests to the blood, and just as the nature of the blood circulation in the body is smooth and flowing, so the hair should be smooth, rich in color, and flowing. It should not be too thick, nor too curly. (Curls transfer the power of the blood to the hair, leaving the body without the nutrition it requires.)

Ideal hair is fair and shiny, soft and wavy, not too oily, and pleasant-smelling. A person with hair like this will succeed in business, and his or her economic and social status will be solid and strong.

Too much hair, or hair that is especially thick, attests to the fact that a large amount of energy is burnt much too fast, and this is manifested in hyperactivity, in power that borders on aggressiveness, in over-sentimentality, and in the rapid waning of the body's energy, leading to early aging, and to a lack of material and spiritual fulfillment.

A bald man has more male energy than female energy, but if the phenomenon is hereditary, there is nothing bad about it, and it is absolutely fine. Baldness, sparse hair, or relatively premature balding are indications of health problems and disruptions in fortune.

In old age, sparse hair attests to good fortune.

The different types of hair also attest to various characteristics according to the following categories:

Fine hair attests to an intelligent, creative person with the soul of an artist. The person has profound thought processes, is romantic, and attributes importance to other people's feelings. He is temperamental and is not daunted by hard work or by taking risks.

Fair, curly hair attests to an intelligent but erratic person who does not persevere in his relationships with the opposite sex, and tends to change jobs frequently. If the hair is particularly frizzy, the person is especially temperamental, and is inclined to be active in a way that is sometimes beyond his capacities.

Very straight hair attests to a compassionate person who is considerate of others. However, this person has no power or perseverance. He generally makes do with the minimum, which means that he has no ambitions, and will not get far. His material and spiritual successes will be very average.

Coarse, rough hair attests to a very impulsive person who does not devote much thought to planning his life. He is liable to fail in business or in his choice of a profession, and is not ensured success in his choice of a mate, either.

Especially fine hair, lacking in volume, attests to an arrogant and superficial person, one who lacks originality and depth of thought, mainly as a result of a lack of confidence. This person is not liked by those around him, and it is difficult for him to create genuine relationships with others. He enjoys flattery, but does not trust those around him, and they in turn are wary of him.

The neck

The neck is the base which supports the head, giving it balance and the ability to function efficiently. The neck is flexible and can expand and contract, and it joins the head to the body. The neck does not contain bones, except for the seven bones at the back that constitute the top end of the spinal column; these are in fact the only bones in the neck. However, the neck consists of many strong muscles that help support the head and hold it erect. The voice is located in the neck, but its strength depends on the entire body and how it breathes.

A loud, clear, resonant voice in any kind of body, even a short and thin one, attests to success in life, since the voice is an indication of presence and of inner strength, which can influence both the person's own activity and others.

When the voice is soft and unclear, its owner has difficulty realizing his ambitions, and his health is poor.

If the person is tall and fat, but his voice is soft and unclear, his condition is bad, and he can expect many disappointments in life, both from the economic point of view and from the social point of view. His life expectancy is low, his health is poor, and he does not consolidate relationships with the members of his family or with friends.

The Adam's apple is not meant to protrude, unless the person is very thin. A protruding Adam's apple in a big, fat person attests to someone whose marriage is unhappy, and to idleness, but it is also an indication of a person who knows how to channel his life; generally speaking, this type gets what he wants.

The shape of the neck indicates the length and quality of a person's life, and what material success and health await him.

The ideal neck is well-shaped, round and solid, medium in size, neither too long nor too short. It is lighter in color than the face and body, and is smooth, straight, without protrusions, and without visible veins. The length of the neck is supposed to be in proportion to the length of the face and the body, and women's necks are generally speaking relatively longer than men's.

A very long neck attests to the fact that its owner is unlucky. He does not have luck in business, and his health is poor.

A short neck and an elongated face indicate that their owner will soon have children.

A long neck and a full body mean a short life.

Four types of neck can be discerned:

The first type is round and smooth. This is a solid, muscular neck, with two horizontal stripes encompassing it. This neck indicates that its owner is healthy, liked by those around him, has a quiet, responsibly organized life, and is romantic in his relations with the opposite sex.

The second type is short and solid. The owner of this neck is an energetic type who is successful and enjoys good profits from his business; he knows how to activate other people for his own purposes, even though sometimes he operates cunningly in order to achieve his objectives.

The third type is thin and flat with no protrusions. The owner of this neck has large-scale ambitions, but is unable to realize them. For this reason, he is greatly frustrated, and this causes him suffering that influences his life.

The fourth type is long, smooth and full. Its owner is an honest person who succeeds in life, but his success stems from positive activity and from his great credibility in his relations with himself and with others. This person tends to engage in artistic pursuits, literature, the humanities, and in studies, and he derives satisfaction from them. He does not seek economic success, nor is he successful in material and economic matters.

The shoulders

Ideal shoulders are supposed to be solid, flat and broad. These shoulders attest to people who have physical and emotional strength, who can cope with life's vicissitudes, and who can attain economic and social achievements.

Conversely, thin, narrow shoulders attest to physical and emotional weakness; their owners are not strong enough to overcome the daily difficulties of earning a living. For this reason, their economic situation is poor, and they can expect health problems.

It is important to note that every type of shoulder can be improved, and the person's physical and emotional condition will improve accordingly.

Round shoulders can be strengthened by appropriate exercises, weight-lifting, and so on. The person should do a lot of exercises that loosen the shoulders in order to straighten and stabilize the spinal column and to hold the neck upright, because then even round shoulders will not harm the physical build. The shoulders can be improved by doing suitable exercises, and this will improve the owner's personality, enhance his positive characteristics, and reinforce his sense of self.

Four types of shoulders can be discerned: thin, narrow

shoulders; hunched, high shoulders; broad, muscular shoulders; and round shoulders.

The first type: Thin, narrow shoulders attest to weakness. Their owner lacks physical strength, but even more important, he lacks the strength to cope with life's vicissitudes, and generally speaking he gives up, but remains frustrated. He engages in occupations which do not require physical effort, and is not crazy about sport. As he is weak, he will not have many children.

This type can improve his shoulders, mainly the muscles, for the sake of his physical welfare, but even more so for the sake of getting his life onto a solid basis. The choice of a sport that is suitable for the shoulders, such as sailing and rowing, appropriate exercises and swimming, will most likely strengthen his shoulder muscles and improve his chances to succeed in life.

The second type: Hunched, high (at the ends furthest from the head) shoulders attest to restlessness. Their owner does not find peace in his life, and as a result is unable to establish himself at work, in his place of residence, or in finding a circle of true, long-standing friends. He tends to do several things at once without completing any of them, and for this reason does not succeed. He is eternally busy, but nothing comes of it.

He is curious by nature, and as a result engages in detective work, science and research, and professions that require studying written material in depth. This fact means that his reading position exacerbates his hunched shoulders (which has repercussions on his character), and causes his characteristics to penetrate deeply into his consciousness and actions.

This type, too, can augment the strength in his shoulders,

which in turn will strengthen his character and body by means of appropriate fitness exercises, such as arm exercises, marksmanship, handstands, and so on.

The third type: Broad, muscular shoulders indicate great power. Their owner is successful both in business and in management. He can cope with life's vicissitudes, deal with situations of both mental and physical stress, and can extricate himself from difficulties. He helps others cope and get out of difficult situations in which they are embroiled. He is self-confident, and his senses are honed and guide him in finding the correct solutions. As he is friendly, other people listen to him and act according to his advice. His sexual relations are excellent, and he gives his partner a lot of satisfaction.

The fourth type: When round shoulders descend in a slope from the neck to their outer edges, they attest to weakness. When they are thick and muscular, they attest to strength and the ability to succeed.

Women with narrow shoulders were always considered more feminine than those with broad shoulders, and in the past, round shoulders in women were considered a sign of beauty and intelligence.

Nowadays, this has changed, and women with thin, round shoulders are not considered successful, perhaps because today broad shoulders are necessary to cope with life's challenges.

It can be discerned that the two members of each pair of shoulders are not altogether identical, and this lack of identity can be seen in two types:

The first type: When the right shoulder is significantly higher than the left, it indicates that the person is conceited, overly pretentious, unable to realize the little things in life because he only goes after big successes - without making too much of an effort to achieve them. He expects success to come chasing after him, which generally does not happen. As a result of his great arrogance, he is not well liked, which means that he cannot avail himself of the help of others in realizing his ambitions.

The second type - in which the left shoulder is significantly higher than the right, indicates that the person is pleasant, considerate toward others, successful in business, and his relations with those around him are friendly. When the left shoulder is exaggeratedly higher than the right, the person is overly generous, and this is his most noticeable characteristic.

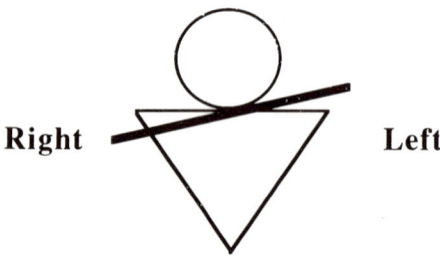

The arms

The arms attest to achievements in life and the person's influence on his surroundings. The ideal length of the arms is half the length of the body. Those are long arms, which can reach far, meaning that they can broaden their owner's sphere of influence.

Round, solid arms are an indication of a high level of professional ability, and of achievement-orientation and the realization of the ability to succeed economically.

The muscles of the arm should be solid, taut, smooth and flexible. When the skin is flaccid and thin, the person lacks good fortune, and is a pale, non-influential type.

The color of the arms should be identical to that of the body, that is, warm and reddish.

The part of the arm from the fingertips to the elbow is called "the dragon's bone," and as it is the dominant part of the arm, it is called "the king."

The second part of the bone, from the elbow to the shoulder, is called "the tiger's bone" and as it is secondary in importance, it is called "the king's minister."

If the tiger's bone is stronger than the dragon's bone, its owner's expectations do not come true, nor are his ambitions realized, a fact which engenders frustration and bitterness that emerge in his relations with the people around him.

There are five types of arms:

If **the arms are far too long and reach the knees**, their owner is extraordinarily successful. There is nothing he cannot achieve; however, he is hardly realistic, and is more suited to being a god than a human being. (In fact, Buddha is usually described as having disproportionately long arms.)

If **the arms are especially long**, the person is blessed with good fortune, he exerts great influence on others, and his range of achievements is also broad. He can attain senior positions, and he has no trouble obtaining whatever he wants.

Short arms are arms that measure less than two fifths of the entire length of the body, and they attest to difficulty in obtaining things. The shorter the arms, the harder it is for them to reach things that are far away, so that their owners have to make an effort in order to obtain the things that life offers. Studies do not come easily to these people, they have to put a lot into their work in order to advance, and their economic situation depends on the effort they make to consolidate it. If they do not attempt to spread themselves over too many professions and fields of interest, but rather concentrate on one area that they like, and go into it in depth, they are likely to be very successful. Their success will evaporate when they try to exceed the boundaries of their abilities, which are in fact limited - but even so, contain many possibilities.

Round, solid, medium-length arms are an indication of a person who has abilities, who adapts readily to his environment, and who generally gets what he wants. This is an open and broad-minded individual, who is involved in society, and he makes many friends easily. He is serious about his work and in his relationship with his mate, and has no inclination for adventures and gambles. His aspirations in life do not exceed his physical and mental capabilities, and therefore he realizes them fully. If he has aspirations, he sees to it that he has the means necessary to fulfill them before he acts.

Flat, thin, medium-length arms indicate difficulties in achieving objectives; these difficulties stem from a weak, inflexible and non-ambitious character. The person dreams about success, but is unable to achieve it. He is afraid of initiatives and changes, and is unable to undertake big things. He lives from day to day, and does not set up clear objectives for himself. When he encounters challenges, he cannot cope with them, and prefers to retreat. He cannot deal with prestigious jobs, does not think himself capable of higher education, and feels that he has not got the power to cope, even though he has the capacity for it.

It should be noted that thin arms can be improved and strengthened by means of suitable exercises, such as rowing, which strengthen the arms and ease the tension in them, and as a result, the body is reinforced and the soul galvanized to action and to facing challenges.

The armpit

Armpit hair and the amount of perspiration in the armpit are also indications of the person's achievement-orientation.

If the person's armpit hair is thick and full, he will be successful, his business will prosper, and his health will be good; however, if the hair is dry and pale, there could be worrisome problems which detract from the person's quality of life. These could be material problems, such as a lack of financial resources with which to accomplish big projects, or even temporary health problems.

Thin, sparse armpit hair is an indication of poor nutrition in the person's youth, and a lack of moral education, culminating in a mature person who is sickly and has defective mental abilities. This kind of person will not go far in life. His sex life will not be satisfying, and he is liable to become afflicted with sexual ailments.

A small amount of perspiration in the armpit is an

indication of a person who knows how to handle his affairs correctly. His investments are wise, and his profits increase.

Excessive perspiration attests to a narrow-minded person who fears conspiracies against him, and does not initiate things or make investments for fear of failure. The health of this person, too, is not good, and he is susceptible to illnesses.

The hands

The hands are an indication of how a person perceives and understands life, and of how he relates to work, money and friends.

There are six types of hands:

The first type - medium-size, soft, smooth and pleasant hands without protrusions or obvious bones. This person is amiable, easy-going, leads a quiet and happy domestic life, and succeeds in business without putting in too much effort.

A woman whose hand is soft and delicate is thought to be warm and gentle, occasionally easily seduced, but generally speaking a caring and protective family person.

The second type - medium-size hands with solid but elastic skin. The person is successful in his affairs and improves everything he does all his life. He is a warm type, kind-hearted, clever, studious, active, and popular with those around him. He is a flexible person who does not miss opportunities that promise to advance his career or lead to achievements.

The third type - hands with thin fingers, protruding bones, and big gaps between them. Their skin is dry, and they are cool to the touch. These hands are an indication of hard work and great effort in an attempt to achieve success.

The person works hard and puts a great deal of physical and emotional effort into building his life. In most cases, he is not helped by anyone on his path to success.

He is an individualist who is not prepared to listen to anyone else's advice, and occasionally he fails to achieve his objectives because of his stubborn insistence on doing things his way.

The fourth type - big, bony hands, almost without the sensation of flesh, with very small gaps between the fingers. These hands indicate hard physical labor rather than mental and intellectual abilities. Although from the physical point of view the person is strong, and hard work brings remuneration, in most cases he has a hard time making decisions, and requires the assistance of others; basically he is a very dependent person.

The fifth type - big, fat hands, flexible and soft, without protruding bones, and small gaps between the fingers. The owner of these hands is successful, creative, and has the soul of an artist. His personality radiates out onto other people, and because of his pleasant and congenial nature, he is well liked. His creations, which are mainly artistic, are well known and bring in commensurate financial rewards.

The sixth type - small, thin hands with wide gaps between the fingers. The owner of these hands is an idealist - generally a scientist, philosopher, author or inventor. He is a very unrealistic type, and daily life is difficult for him. He finds it hard to cope with materialism, and it is hard for him to apply his ideas because of impracticality and materialistic inflexibility. He is overflowing with ideas, but fails to implement them. He cannot create a firm economic basis, and his life is difficult as a result.

Hand colors

In general, the ideal hand color is pink, as it is an indication of great financial ability. Conversely, shades of yellow attest to financial weakness and poor health.

Red - indicates great wealth.
Pink - indicates financial success and high status.
Pinkish-yellowish - indicates difficulties in obtaining money.
Greenish - indicates poor health.
Whitish - indicates a pessimistic nature, poor health and depression, but if these hands are flexible or fat, their owners are optimistic and do not sink into deep depressions.
Yellow - indicates poor health and financial difficulties.

Hands should be massaged in order to strengthen them and improve their flexibility, mainly because the major part of personal success resides in them. Solid, flexible hands are a testimony to clever, serious, and alert thinking, to a creative soul, to high morale, and to an easy-going nature - things that govern material success and a high-quality domestic and social life.

The fingers

There are five types of fingers:

The first type - These are long, delicate, pointed fingers with big gaps between them. They indicate sensitivity, individuality and curiosity. This type of person is conceited, arrogant, selfish, and enjoys life. He is very impulsive and does not relate to other people's feelings. He is an intellectual, and does not like to work hard.

The second type - These fingers have bony protrusions in their joints, indicating a person of great intelligence and an intellectual with excellent analytical powers. People with these fingers are successful in academic professions, research and science. They derive a great deal of satisfaction from their professions, and even if they do not become rich, their academic world satisfies them.

The third type - Square fingers attest to a practical, highly predictable, systematic and persistent person. He is honest and reliable, and can be trusted. He likes helping others, but as he is stubborn, he does not compromise. Because of his high degree of self-confidence, he is not prepared to accept other people's opinions.

The fourth type - A large, round palm, with round fingers indicates a simple, superficial and hasty person, whose actions are governed by impulse rather than by logical considerations. He does not weigh his moves carefully, and is liable to run into problems very easily, without knowing how to cope with them. He can cause damage unwittingly. Since this kind of person is very superficial, he cannot engage in occupations that demand knowledge and thought, and tends to do simple manual labor that does not ensure any kind of economic basis for the future. As he is unpredictable, he is liable to get embroiled in awkward situations from which it is difficult to extricate himself.

The fifth type - This person has smooth, narrow fingers, which attest to the soul of an artist, to sensitivity and creativity. Since he is impatient, he is inconsiderate of other people's feelings, and is critical; generally speaking, he is dissatisfied both with what he does and with what others do. He is selfish, spoilt, and egocentric. This kind of person tends to engage in art, music or writing.

The fingernails

There are three types of fingernails:

The first type - Short, flat fingernails indicate health problems in the stomach - especially in the digestive system - which manifest themselves in stomach-aches.

The second type - Round, convex fingernails indicate heart and other health problems, especially heart attacks and respiratory problems.

The third type - Narrow fingernails indicate slow metabolism, which causes fatigue, weakness, and susceptibility to disease.

The color of the fingernails attest to their owner's state of health; when they are pink, the owner is healthy.

Smooth fingernails are an indication of strength and stability of the body and soul.

If the fingernails are gray, their owner is on the way to heart and lung problems.

Diagonal or vertical lines on the fingernails are a sign of rapid aging, or of defective blood circulation.

To increase the rate of blood circulation, the fingertips should be massaged in order to open the capillaries.

The chest

The chest is linked to achievement and the ability to cope with life. It is worth noting that when the chest muscles are developed, they bestow health and strength. However, when they are flaccid, the person can expect health problems. The chest muscles in any type of body, and at any age, can be improved. Developing the chest muscles improves the person's appearance, but more importantly improves his attitude to life, his ability to cope with the problems that face him, and his mood.

There are four types of chests:

The first type - A broad, thick, protruding chest indicates a healthy, strong, active and achievement-oriented person.

Sparse hair on a man's chest shows determination, perseverance, and, consequently, the realization of aspirations. This man is successful if he engages in sport, in a military career, and so on. If the hair is smooth, silky and pleasant to look at, the person's success is assured.

In a woman, a large, broad chest is an indication of a positive attitude and optimism. This woman knows how to cope with the vicissitudes of life, and come out on top. In general, this is a career-oriented woman, who operates among strong men, but is not afraid of competing with them; she does so gracefully but firmly. As for beauty - well, it lies in the eye of the beholder...

The second type - A flat, narrow chest is an indication of a poetic soul and spiritual strength. Generally speaking, this person is introverted, does not make friends easily, and prefers to delve into his own affairs rather than deal with those of other people. This type of person is creative and very imaginative, and engages in literature, poetry, science, research, or other art forms.

The third type - A full, round chest is an indication of activity, adventurousness and risk-taking, which do not help the person fully accomplish the missions he sets himself. However, since he is a pleasant, non-aggressive type, it does not affect his conduct, and he achieves his medium-level objectives. He is sociable and well-liked, nice-looking, and his relationship with his spouse is warm.

The fourth type - An average chest, with pleasant, round outlines, neither too big nor too small. Its owner is a gentle, responsible, but not independent person. He depends on others, and does not initiate things. He is the type of person who implements the things he is instructed to do with total responsibility. He is friendly and well-liked, but not assertive, and therefore not ambitious. He is satisfied with a peaceful life, and with a profession that brings in a respectable income, but high-ranking jobs or management positions are not for him.

The breasts

In a woman, the breasts symbolize motherhood. They are an indication of the number of children she will have, and of the kind of mother she will be. They belong to the yin cosmic energy, which is expressed in femininity, motherhood, and, most importantly, in a certain submissiveness that engenders dependence on her spouse.

It should be noted that breasts can be improved, molded and strengthened, which will have immediate effect on the woman's emotional strength and ability to stick up for her principles. Massaging the breasts stimulates blood circulation, and increases the amount of energy that is stored in them, at the same time releasing tensions and pressures. It also shapes the breasts, which are a powerful focus of sexual attraction.

Massaging the breasts is done when the woman is lying on her back, or while washing herself. First the fingers massage the nipples gently, and then massage the area around the nipples in small circular movements. The circumference of the circular movements gradually increases as the movements progress from the center toward the sides, and then decreases as the movements return to the nipples.

With men, the breasts are a symbol of fertility and of the number of children he will father. The man's nipples are the buds of future children, and if they are big, they indicate many children.

If there is a little bit of hair on the nipples, the man's fertility is ensured, but when they are very hairy, his fertility is defective.

The best color for a man's aureoles is reddish brown, and the nipple itself should be a dark red.

The woman's breasts are one of her centers of sexuality, which is why they attract men. However, their main function is feeding infants, and they represent the woman's chances of giving birth, and her motherliness.

There are six types of women's breasts:

The first type - This is characterized by flat, circular breasts. A woman who has breasts of this kind is conservative, home-loving, clean and tidy. She is clever and pleasant, but sometimes withdrawn. This type of woman tends to marry a man who can support her well, and she handles the domestic front skillfully. In most cases, she gives birth to two children, but not before she has ensured that she has the means to give them a good upbringing. She raises her children meticulously and didactically, adhering to a course of action which prepares them for coping with life's vicissitudes.

The second type - These breasts are round and full, like inverted bowls. They indicate a healthy woman, a faithful spouse, and a good mother to equally healthy children.

This woman is clever, and takes good care of the members of her household. However, as she is passionate and selfish, she is not prepared to sacrifice anything for the sake of her children. She raises them and provides them with everything they need - up to the point that she thinks they can stand on their own two feet. From the moment she has decided that they are ready to face life, she stops giving, as she is very acquisitive, and is concerned about her personal welfare. She loves her children, and wants the best for them, but not at her expense, and without excessive personal sacrifice on her part.

The third type - These breasts are round and bouncy, and are an indication of an extremely fertile woman. However, she generally does not give birth to many children, as they are liable to interfere with her way of life. This kind of woman loves having a good time, is often career-oriented, and her numerous interets are more important to her than being cooped up with her children. She is not willing to sacrifice herself, either for her children or for her husband. Her frequent absences from home can lead to rows between her and her husband, and domestic life can run into trouble.

If her nipples are big, she will disappear from her home for an extended period, neglecting the members of her family for the sake of her own pleasures, possibly even infidelities.

The fourth type - These breasts push upward. A woman of this type is very fertile, pleasant, congenial, optimistic and smiling. However, she is also arrogant, and is prone to mood-swings. This side of her character engenders many conflicts between her and the rest of her family, and undermines the peaceful well-being that generally prevails among them.

The fifth type - These are ball-like breasts that spread outward. They are full, and indicate early puberty and marriage. Women with these breasts are quick to settle down, and tend to gain weight at a young age. They are ambitious and want to succeed in life. They galvanize their spouses to action, giving them full moral support, while they see to the running of the household. They are faithful wives who create a warm domestic atmosphere. They bring up their children with love and devotion, and encourage them to succeed.

The sixth type - Women with hanging, oval breasts suffer from poor nutrition which engenders susceptibility to disease and a lack of physical immunity.

A woman with breasts of this kind gives birth to many children, but has a hard time raising them, not only because of her physical weakness, but also because of her spinelessness, her melancholy nature, and her tendency toward depression. She is dependent, and as she does not have any financial sources of her own, she nullifies herself vis-a-vis those around her.

The back

The back indicates reserves of physical strength as well as the capacity for profitability and wealth. The ideal back is strong and muscular, and radiates power and stability, which are a vital basis for success and achievement in life.

In addition, a strong back attests to shrewdness and wisdom, but also to a high degree of intelligence and the ability to act wisely and sometimes slyly in delicate situations.

The back is male cosmic energy, or yang, and it extends from the shoulders to the waist, with the spinal column located vertically in the center. The ancient Chinese attributed great importance to the spine, and saw it as the channel of the life force.

If the back is straight, its owner is ensured health and many children; however, if it is crooked, its owner will have a hard time making his way in life, as he can expect problems with health and income, and he will have trouble fathering children.

In fact, back problems are widespread among a large portion of the population, which has different types of backs, and these problems can be attributed to the heavy weight that backs support. Strong back muscles can prevent these problems, and developing these muscles is a key to a healthy back.

Every form of exercise that strengthens the back muscles and enhances the shape of the back is highly recommended!

There are four types of backs:

The first type - A broad back, which indicates strength and achievement-orientation. A person with a back of this kind can cope with power struggles and win them, and is likely to obtain high-ranking jobs and managerial positions. However, he is also a helpful and supportive type, who protects his family and the people close to him.

The second type - A back that is rounded like a dome is an indication of business acumen, success, and wealth. As these people are flexible by nature, they are good at conducting negotiations, and usually make their way to the top by exploiting their manipulative abilities.

The more economic power they accumulate, the more they enjoy the good life, and indulge in fine food - but they also gain a significant amount of weight. As they do not participate in athletic activities, they are clumsy in adolescence and their health is undermined.

The third type - A triangular back, broad at the top and narrowing toward the waist, indicates a creative, sensual, amiable, and well-liked person who enjoys a reasonable standard of living, and provides for his family, even though he does not aspire to senior positions. A member of the middle class, he takes care of his wife and children and enjoys his life, but does not have great ambitions, provided that his needs and those of his family are fulfilled.

As these types of people are flexible, they are generally mobile, and are not afraid of long work trips, or even going from one country to the next if their livelihood depends on it.

The fourth type - A thin, narrow back indicates a person who is not healthy. In addition to back and spinal problems, this person is a dreamy type who does not see reality as it is. They do not pursue material things, but rather a spiritual and artistic life. They are mainly painters, musicians, writers, researchers, or academics. They are artistically gifted, but usually have to struggle to make a living. The outstanding ones among them - the virtuosi - are those who succeed financially. Most of these types live frugally, and focus their interest on spiritual development.

The waist

The waist is the area which divides the body into the upper torso and the lower torso. The diaphragm is the borderline, and the waist is the narrowest part of this region.

The waist is responsible for the unique nature of the

person. It indicates the uniqueness of the person in life, and his personal initiative.

The ideal waist is taut, long and round. It ensures health and wealth when the entire diaphragm is built in a strong and proportionate way. The material and emotional life of a person with this diaphragm is balanced, his decisions are carefully weighed up, and the wide range of opportunities available enables him to make the correct and successful choice of direction in life, leading ultimately to a high economic and social status.

The personal advancement of the individual depends, therefore, on how his waist is built. He has to work at acquiring a long, solid build for his waist, and watch his health and posture. In this way he can induce the life strength in him to move in the direction of success.

In general, there are two types of waists:

Type A - muscular, solid and flexible.
Type B - fat and fleshy.

Remember that the waist can be shaped and improved; by doing the appropriate exercises, this can be accomplished relatively quickly.

A finer analysis reveals four typical kinds of waists:

The first type - A thin, narrow waist indicates a person lacking in self-confidence and initiative, dependent on others, and with a passive personality. This person cannot fight and overcome obstacles. He has trouble earning a living, as well as social problems. He is mentally unstable, and without the right help is liable to deteriorate.

The second type - A round waist attests to a happy person who is contented with his lot. Economically, he has a solid basis and makes a respectable living. The main weakness of this type resides in sudden outbursts about unimportant things, which are liable to engender irrational reactions. However, as he is generally stable, he can pull himself together and emerge fortified from these crises.

The third type - A flat waist without any indentation is an indication of poor health, financial instability, and few children. This person is creative, and is likely to succeed as an artist or a man of letters. However, he lacks energy, and his activities will mainly be devoid of obvious inspiration.

The fourth type - A shapely, narrow waist is an indication of powerful sexuality. People like this are active, fun-loving and athletic. They are not serious, and prefer to live for the moment rather than devise long-term plans. They do not make any effort to obtain jobs that will ensure a respectable income, and do not aspire to an established and serious domestic life. They are very easy-going people, which means that their success in life is doubtful and entirely fortuitous.

The abdomen

The abdomen is an indication of wealth and status in life. The upper part of the abdomen is smaller than the lower part, and the veins should not protrude.

The ideal abdomen for both men and women is round, full, elastic and sinking downward slightly - something like the abdomen of a women in her first months of pregnancy - neither thin nor flat. This kind of abdomen is a sign of longevity, wealth and a respectable station in society.

Seeing that the abdomen houses the fetus during pregnancy (in women, of course!), it should be muscular in order to bear the weight of the fetus. If it is slack, it impairs the efficient functioning of the intestines.

The navel, which is the central point of the abdomen, is connected with fertility, and it should be concave rather than protruding. The more concave it is, the greater the number of children.

In order to strengthen the abdominal muscles, swimming, rowing and bicycle-riding are recommended. In addition, appropriate fitness exercises can strengthen the lower back and help to strengthen the abdomen.

There are four types of abdomens:

The first type - A round abdomen, slightly fallen and not taut, is a sign of success and health.

The fashion today is different, and a flat abdomen, especially for women, is considered preferable. In former times, however, a fallen abdomen was considered a sign of generosity and an easier, freer life.

The second type - A big, protruding abdomen is an indication of great wealth, but also of vulgarity and coarseness. People with this kind of abdomen own vast amounts of property, but generally lack taste, and they display their abundant wealth in a cheap and vulgar manner. They use their money for their personal ends only, but unsuccessfully, as it does not ensure their future. They do not contribute to the good of other people. Their character is weak, sometimes corrupt and lazy. During adolescence, they suffer from physical problems as a result of laziness and overeating.

The third type - A high, pointed abdomen attests to a restless person who tries his hand at various occupations, but never completes anything. He works hard, but does not achieve the desired results. Despite his never-ending efforts, he does not attain high positions, and his income is limited. His life is difficult, and as he grows older, he is likely to have health problems. He ages rapidly.

The fourth type - A flat abdomen is an indication of a spiritual person with the soul of an artist. He is intelligent, but is unable to realize his aspirations in life because of his spaced-out nature. From the financial point of view, his situation is generally bad. He is very spontaneous, but he is not focused, nor is he able to stick to a permanent job.

The genitals

The genitals are meant primarily for procreation, but also for the satisfaction of sensual desire and as an expression of love.

The ideal masculine sex organ is medium in length, with a short, round, slightly flat head; this ensures great fertility and numerous offspring.

An organ which is either too long or too short is insufficiently fertile.

The testicles should be warm and dark, solid and wrinkled, with thin strips that guarantee many children.

As for the female sex organ, if its labia protrude, its inner area is soft and pink, and the hair surrounding it is smooth, the woman will have a strong, healthy husband, a good domestic life, a respectable income, and strong children. If the uterine aperture protrudes, the woman will have a respected social and economic position.

If pubic hair grows at a young age, it is an indication of a short life. Sparse hair indicates high fertility and a lot of children. A satisfying sex life is ensured when the pubic hair is soft and abundant.

There are four types of pubic hair:

The first type - Long hair in a diamond shape is the most masculine of all, attesting to strength, energy, and vitality. This type of pubic hair can also be found in women.

The second type - Short hair in a diamond shape is an indication of a slightly lesser degree of masculinity. This type of pubic hair can also be found in women.

The third type - Hair in a triangular shape attests to an average degree of femininity. Both sexes can have this type of pubic hair.

The fourth type - Hair in the shape of two half moons attests to the highest degree of femininity. This type of pubic hair is found only in women.

While the main emphasis on the vitality of the genitals is procreation, the ancient Chinese attributed a great deal of importance to the sexual side, which is the motivating life force. It is also a sign of economic success, social clout, health, longevity, and the establishment of a homogeneous family.

The Chinese believe in the correct (not exaggerated) amount of sexual relations, as only by exercising moderation can success in all areas be assured. Overindulgence in sexual intercourse is liable to bring about diseases, tensions, economic and mental instability, and a short life-span. The life force should be exploited for the right purposes, in the correct amounts, and energy that should be directed toward more important objectives should not be wasted.

The male and female energies complement each other, and they should be balanced in the world. This balance ensures intellectual and emotional success.

The thighs and buttocks

The thighs and buttocks constitute the body's center of movement, and in the broader sense, indicate how a person functions, and how he navigates his path through life.

Since the thighs and buttocks play an important role in the body, care must be taken to stabilize and strengthen them physically. Appropriate exercises can improve them. Swimming, jogging, walking, and every type of sport which entails movement are effective in improving their degree of fitness.

It is difficult to lose excess weight in these areas, but regular exercise can help.

There are five types of thighs and buttocks:

The first type - balanced. The thighs are medium in size, the buttocks are slightly round, and the pelvic bone provides balanced support for them. This structure is an indication of serenity, self-confidence, and stability. The person is warm and well-liked, and leads a healthy life from every point of view.

These people lead good domestic lives and raise healthy children. They are intellectuals, who have profound thought processes and open minds. Their economic future is certain, and they attain senior positions as a result of their talents, perseverance and stability. They navigate their way through life with no difficulty, as they know how to manage and how to avoid obstacles and extreme situations.

The second type - Round thighs and buttocks attest to people who are determined, uncompromising, and idealistic, and who espouse high principles. These people are happy, passionate and good at business, and their financial status is excellent. They enjoy life, and are well-liked by those around them. Although their station in life is not among society's elite, it is sufficiently respectable, and they are satisfied and contented with their lot.

They navigate their way through life by swimming in rough waters, where they are compelled to cope with stormy waves, but they extricate themselves from the difficulties, and reach their destination.

The third type - Flat thighs and buttocks are an indication of high intelligence, of lofty ambitions, but also of great naivety. These people are incapable of making money, but conversely, they are not interested in materialism.

They slide along the paths of life without defined aims or ambitions. They go with the flow, and roll along in whichever direction the wind blows. They have no difficulty with moving house or changing jobs according to whatever comes along - they just keep hoping that life will direct them safely to shore.

A woman with this build is not fertile, and she gives birth to few children.

The fourth type - Broad thighs and ample buttocks are an indication of health, a romantic soul, the ability to give love, but also a certain degree of selfishness. These people do not hesitate to use all and any means to accomplish their objectives, but they are usually pleasant, considerate, and financially successful.

They navigate their way through life by repressing problems and ignoring them, their aim being economic profitability and material stability. They are not interested in prestige and fame - only in a strong financial basis.

The fifth type - Raised thighs and upward-protruding buttocks indicate a tendency to give, especially in the sexual realm. These people are well-liked, and they know how to pamper and give credit where it is due. They have a very strong life force, which can not only withstand life's crises and disappointments successfully, but can emerge from them fortified.

They navigate their way through life by hopping and skipping and landing themselves in traps, but they can jump high enough to get out of them. They take care of themselves, and lead comfortable lives without too many worries. Sometimes they are careless, as they live according to their own yardsticks, and not according to reality, which sometimes demands cutbacks or change. This is why they do not attain high status - but this does not worry them particularly.

The legs

The legs indicate action, and promote success and achievements in life. The ideal legs are short and solid, and the person is an intellectual type whose achievements reside in the humanities, both in teaching and in research.

Legs with sparse hair, with the exception of the inner thighs, are an indication of people who are exceptionally successful and fortunate.

Because of the great importance of the legs, their fitness should be improved, as should that of the whole body. The legs constitute a serious action center for the body; the very act of walking is an activity, and it is done without any particular preparation.

Even so, it is good to do a lot of swimming, running, and sports which entail movement.

In addition, stomach exercises, such as push-ups and breathing exercises, also help the legs.

There are three types of legs:

The first type - Straight, taut, strong legs indicate success in life which occurs in the person's forties or fifties.

A person of this type is financially stable, and accumulates property during his life. His domestic life is also good.

If he has short legs, his success will be in the intellectual realm, but if his legs are long, he has impressive physical abilities and can be a successful sportsman, a talented workman, a farmer or an industrialist.

The second type - Thin, bony legs attest to little ambition and non-realization of aspirations.

These legs are an indication of mobility, and the people tend to move house and change jobs. It is difficult for them to settle down and establish themselves, as they are characterized by a lack of stability. Because of their mobility, these people are inclined to engage in occupations that require a lot of movement and travel, such as salesmen, journalists, or seamen, and as a result of their wanderings, they start anew within brief time-spans, even before completing the previous period. By maturity, they have not succeeded in settling down, nor have they attained status or security.

The third type - Fat, broad upper thighs, becoming narrow in the knee region and down to the lower part of the leg. The owner of these legs is not an active person, and his success in life comes to the fore at a late age. His family life is good, and his relations with the members of his household are warm and pleasant. His spouse is the one who occasionally lays the burden of livelihood and future economic basis on his shoulders, while he himself is satisfied with the short-term view of obtaining the things that are needed on a daily basis.

The feet

The feet indicate their owner's standing in life, his stability and his ability to get a respectable job.

As a person ages, the soles of the feet become hard, so it is very important to take care of them by massaging them. Likewise, the toes must be looked after. The baby toe especially must be massaged, as it is the seat of sexuality, which is the most significant life energy.

The ideal feet are solid, not too bony and not too thin. They are flexible and shapely. They should be in proportion to the rest of the body, and when the big toe is short and the person's physical build is thin, the person is fortunate.

A high arch indicates a high level of achievement, while a flat foot attests to the inability to attain senior positions.

The color of the foot is generally lighter than that of the body, and the heel should have numerous wrinkles, as this is an indication of the accumulation of a great deal of property.

If there are gaps between the toes, and the second toe is longer than the big toe, it is a sign of being athletically gifted.

People with long toes are generally stable, and usually remain in the same place of residence and the same job for a long time, while people with short toes are generally restless, and tend to move house and change jobs frequently. This means that they have difficulty establishing themselves.

Sparse hair on the toes is an indication of the energy and temperament that are necessary for winning the competition for jobs and success in life.

There are four types of feet:

The first type - Long narrow feet mean that the person is fortunate, and will attain high positions and excellent social and economic status.

The second type - Short, broad feet indicate hard-working people who toil all their lives for a living, but because of their tendency to be dependent, they are unable to make decisions, and need to be directed. They usually lean on their spouses, who have to bear the heavy burden, and they are frustrated with their poor abilities.

The third type - Flat feet are an indication of a miserable childhood, and of instability, which is manifested in a lack of perseverance, in the inability to make social and economic contacts, and in the inability to attain senior positions. This person's life is difficult, he barely earns a living, and his domestic life is shaky.

The fourth type - Broad, flat feet attest to an inability to get off the ground. This kind of person is very earthy, very attached to the earth and his roots, not intellectual, and succeeds only at manual labor. He is not destined for studies beyond basic, compulsory education.

The heel

The wrinkles on the heel are also significant in predicting a person's future. Heels can be divided into the following types:

The first type - Unwrinkled heels attest to a lack of wisdom, a lack of wit, and a very low intellectual capacity.

The second type - Many wrinkles are a sign of great literary ability and broad intellectual knowledge.

The third type - "Round" wrinkles are a promise of fame and acknowledgment in society.

The fourth type - Wrinkles that are etched in a shapely, well-matched way are a sign of abundant material wealth.

The fifth type - Deep wrinkles attest to developed intellectual ability, and an ability for in-depth studies, but they also indicate a covetous nature. In spite of this, the person will not succeed in becoming rich, and at most will enjoy a reasonable standard of living.

The skin

The skin is, in fact, the largest organ in the body, and it fulfills many functions: It regulates body temperature, protects the internal organs, and excretes perspiration. The upper layer of skin contains dead cells which are constantly regenerated as new cells are created, providing protection against dryness, heat, wind and cold, until they themselves die, and so on.

The sense of touch is also located in the skin, and therefore it is important to look after the skin by washing it and nourishing it with suitable creams and lotions.

The color and texture of the skin relate to the five elements in nature:

Fire - Reddish skin color; dry, cold and rough skin.

Wood - Gray-greenish, olive skin color; dry, taut and smooth skin.

Metal - Ivory skin color; fine, smooth skin.

Water - Dark skin color; moist and slightly puffy skin.

Earth - Golden skin color; rough, hard skin.

The person's success in life, and his state of health and mental condition can be seen in the differences in color between a number of body parts:

The **ears** should be lighter than the color of the face.

The **face** should be darker than the color of the body.

The **neck** should be paler than the face and the body.

The **shoulders** should be identical in color to the body, but ideally they should be warm in color.

Moles

The skin should be free of blemishes, moles or any other marks.

Having said this, moles attest to a fortunate person if they are located in hidden parts of the body and not on the face or on exposed areas, except for moles on the forehead, which promise senior positions (but also indicate marital problems).

There are moles that are very advantageous:

Moles on the palm of the hand and on the heels ensure an excellent economic situation.

Moles on the chest and stomach also attest to great economic and intellectual achievements.

Moles on the genitals are a sign of fertility and many children.

We will now examine special signs in the body:

Bulging eyes - indicate economic problems in a person's forties.

Bulging nostrils - indicate the inability to earn money, or the tendency to lose it.

Protruding ears - indicate an oppressed childhood, the lack of vital necessities, and deprivation of parental love.

Protruding teeth - indicate problems with health and livelihood in old age.

A sunken chin - indicates the inability to attain a job which brings in a satisfactory income.

CHAPTER THREE

TECHNIQUES FOR BALANCING THE BODY

Harmony forms the basis of the Chinese theory. It is achieved by means of the cosmic energies that operate in nature. The more the body approaches this harmony, the more the its physical and mental condition improves.

The ancient Chinese technique combines the analysis of the function of the body as a single unit with the individual treatment of each separate organ, and it supplies vitality to the body, effects impressive self-expression, provides the confidence and strength to accomplish tasks and achievements, preserves the health of the mind and body, and enables the person to reach old age without unnecessary crises.

The basis of the Chinese technique lies in the theory that a balanced body can reach impressive achievements, the final aim being a body that is in harmony with itself and with the world. This is accomplished by means of augmenting vitality and energy by releasing pressures and channeling the energies into positive and beneficial activities. A body that is not naturally balanced can be improved and can accomplish things which provide it with maximum equilibrium.

These techniques are easy to perform, and provide flexibility, release from pressures, body-shaping, and a good feeling, all of which ultimately lead to the efficient functioning of the body in all aspects of life.

Many of the exercises do not require taking time off from daily activities. They can be performed while sitting in the office, during a business meeting, while watching TV, or traveling on a bus, or for a few minutes in the morning after getting out of bed. After bathing, a few minutes are required for exercising. No instruments are needed, and the exercises are simple and easy. These are the exercises which do not demand especially profound thought.

Most people engage in some kind of sporting activity, so these exercises are a supplement to the regular fitness-increasing activities, and constitute an additional helpful factor in the functioning of the body. They are even suitable for people who are disabled and cannot perform standard keep-fit exercises.

Body-shaping
by means of exercises

Our modern lives are action-packed, and the time that is left over for sport and keep-fit exercises is limited. The exercises that are recommended here are not a substitute for conventional fitness exercises, but as they are performed during everyday activities, they can be done easily - and moreover, they treat every part of the body. It has already been mentioned that for disabled people, this kind of exercise is sometimes the only solution for physical activity, as it is easy and very effective.

While the exercises should be performed early in the

morning, since they prepare the body for a busy and action-packed day, they can also be done in the evening, and in this way will ensure lightness and release for people who are accustomed to going out and enjoying night life. Having said this, any time is suitable for performing the exercises, as the result is release from pressures, additional vitality, and a generally improved feeling.

Daily exercise on a permanent basis shapes the body, creates a comfortable disposition and a good feeling, and draws out the person's inner beauty, without any connection to his physical appearance.

There is no need for a special room in which to do the exercises, nor are special accessories, instruments or even specialized training necessary; the exercises are easy for everyone to do.

We suggest eight exercises for the improvement of physical and mental health.

The first exercise
This exercise is used for strengthening and "emptying" the head.

Sit cross-legged with your arms close to the sides of your body. Keep your back straight and your mouth closed. Tap your fingers in circular motions around your lips, gums and teeth. Clasp your hands behind your neck, and let your head lean forward. Unclasp your hands and massage the back of your neck in an upward direction using the surface of the pads of your fingers. Continue doing this exercise until you feel a sense of relief in your head, and your neck becomes red. Place your pinkie in your ear, and your middle finger on the bone behind your ear. Place your index finger on your middle finger, and slide it by pressing downward along the third finger. This pressing-sliding activates the bone of the ear.

The second exercise

This exercise promotes flexibility in the bones of the neck, strengthens them, releases the neck and strengthens the eye muscles.

Sit on a chair with your feet on the floor. Stretch your arms forward, clasp your hands together, then place your fists on your knees. Lean your head backward, and then turn it to the left, with your eyes looking over your left shoulder. Then turn your head to the right, with your eyes looking over your right shoulder.

Repeat the exercise.

The third exercise

This exercise promotes flexibility in the shoulder joints and in the head, neck and upper back muscles, and also releases the chest muscles.

Sit or stand, and lean your head backward. Direct your eyes to the right, and swing your left arm forward and backward. While your head is still leaning back, swing your right arm forward and backward.

While your head is still leaning back, repeat the action with both hands at the same time, first forward and then backward.

The fourth exercise

The purpose of this exercise is to briefly close the mouth and the anus simultaneously, and to extend this sealing process from one minute to three minutes, in order to accumulate and preserve life force.

This exercise enhances stamina and sexual prowess, and promises youthfulness and vitality even during adulthood and old age.

Stand with your legs slightly apart for balance. Close your mouth, place the tip of your tongue on the roof of your mouth, and remain in this position.

Exert internal pressure on your buttocks so as to close your anus, simultaneously contracting your stomach muscles. While your mouth and anus are sealed, massage your kidneys (in the lower back region above your buttocks) with the palms of your hands.

Relax. Repeat the exercise.

The fifth exercise

This exercise aims at strengthening the tongue and improving the swallowing mechanism.

Place your tongue on the roof of your mouth and keep your mouth closed. It fills with saliva. Count to 20 and swallow the saliva.

Repeat this exercise several times.

The sixth exercise

This exercise strengthens the toes and the muscles of the sole of the foot.

Standing, lying down or seated, lift your big toe, at the same time pushing your second toe downward.

Change directions, pushing your big toe downward and lifting the second toe.

Repeat this exercise many times.

Invigorating skin care

Below are two exercises that are meant for improving and caring for the skin; moreover, they refresh the body and make it supple. You should perform them in the middle of your work-day, when you become fatigued and would like to freshen up; this serves as a substitute for a refreshing shower.

The seventh exercise

This exercise is especially successful as a stimulating

warm-up before engaging in sport, or after a sporting activity, to relax and refresh the body. However, it can also be performed independently of any other sporting activity.

This is a refreshing massage exercise, which stimulates blood circulation, increases energy and leaves the skin fresh and supple.

Rub your hands together to warm them. Rub your whole body with your hands. Stop every now and then to rub your hands together to warm them until the entire body massage has been completed.

The eighth exercise

Dip a towel into cold or lukewarm water and wring it out. Roll it up into a rope. Move the rope over your neck, over your back, over your thighs and over the whole posterior region of your body in order to stimulate the action of your skin. Open the towel and wipe your entire body.

Balancing the body by means of pressure massage

According to the ancient Chinese theory, the origin of the body's health, serenity, wisdom, and vitality lies in the balance of the cosmic energies. When the yin and the yang are balanced, a harmony is created that forms the basis of everything in the universe, and among other things, it activates the coordinated functioning of all the parts of the body.

This equilibrium is achieved by means of a number of methods, such as: vitality exercises, correct bathing procedures, suitable nutrition, increased action of the body's senses, various methods of meditation, and the massage of particular body points and folds.

The cosmic energies flow through the body via a number of meridians, which are marked as yin or yang.

The massage of these areas by means of moving a finger along the meridians in circular motions, or treating specific points, stimulates the energy flow and balances the energies for improved functioning of the body.

Pressure points called *tsubo yin* or *tsubo yang*, according to their function, are located along these meridians. Energy is released in these points, and enhances the functioning of the body, increasing the rate of its action. Yang points enhance the body's vitality, while yin points provide it with the necessary balancing serenity.

Massage techniques

There are three methods of pressure massage: Moving a finger along the meridians, circular massage movements along the meridians or points, and pressure on the points. Each one of them aims to accomplish a different objective, but it is possible to switch between them if the person being treated feels that one is more effective than another.

In general, during the treatment, the yin meridians in the inner part of the arms, the legs and the front of the body must be massaged. The yang meridians in the outer part of the body, arms and legs must be massaged from the top down.

Strong pressure should be exerted on the yang meridian, but the treatment of the yin meridian should be as gentle as possible.

Massage by moving a finger

This massage is performed with pressure from a finger which is moved along the meridians. It is easy and preferable for another person to perform this massage, but it can be done without assistance, especially on the front part of the body. The pressure on the yang meridians must be strong but sure, so ideally these meridians should be massaged with the thumb or second finger - even using the third finger to increase the pressure by pushing on the second finger.

The pressure on the yin meridians must be very gentle and constant, so the massage of these meridians should be performed with the middle finger, or with the surface at the back of the three fingers when they are held closely together.

Circular massage

This massage is performed on the meridians and the pressure points. The finger is pressed on the area, and the massage proceeds in circular movements.

Massage of the points

The thumb or the middle finger should be used to massage the main points.

For yin points, the thumb should be used to press on the points for a few seconds, in order to create a gentle but consistent pressure.

The yang points must be pressed for a few seconds with the second finger, using the third finger to increase the pressure by pushing on the second finger.

The number of times that the points can be pressed is limitless, and can be done at any time of the day. It is, however, preferable to do it early in the morning or before going to sleep at night, as well as while bathing, but if you have a very busy day, you can take a break during work and press a few times.

The treatment of the points on the face should be performed in conjunction with skin care, applying moisture and nourishment to the skin after the exercise.

Of course, in order to massage the meridians or the tsubo points using one or other of the methods described above, you have to be familiar with the meridians and points.

Massage of the fingers

According to the ancient Chinese method, a person's youthfulness continues as long as his fingers and toes are flexible and in good condition. When they become stiff, the person ages.

Therefore, daily massage of the fingers and toes helps preserve youthfulness.

Massaging the fingers is easy to do, and can be done at any free moment. You should massage your hands at least once a day.

The stages in massaging the fingers:

Massage the fingers of one hand separately, using the other hand. Tap and stroke every part of the finger that is being treated.

Repeat the massage using circular movements for enhancing the vibration. This will increase the rate of blood circulation.

Squeeze the tip of the thumb and the second finger together for a few seconds, and release. Do this a few times in order to increase and improve the rate of blood circulation.

Rotate each finger backward and forward a few times.

Bend each finger backward and forward in the direction of the joint a few times.

Alternatively, open and close each hand several times, with the fingers taut and stretched out as widely as possible.

Shake each hand in turn several times.

How to massage the toes:

Using your thumb, press each toe from one end to the other. This action not only increases the rate of blood circulation in the individual toe, but it is good for the circulation in the whole body.

Tap along the length of every toe on all sides several times, and then repeat the action using circular movements.

Press the area between the first and second toes.

Clasp the area between the first and second toes, and rotate each of these toes several times, separately, in all directions.

Move the toes forward and backward several times.

The pressure points

There are about 700 tsubo points in the body. These points constitute the focus of the energy currents that flow along the meridians.

Since several meeting points, in addition to being the junctions for localized energy, are responsible for the functioning of the entire body in specific fields, massaging them is likely to improve the functioning of the entire body.

As we mentioned before, each point can be massaged separately, or as a part of the massage of the meridians, but it must be remembered that in both possibilities, the massage must be performed gently and with a constant pressure when the points are yin, increasing the degree of pressure when the points are yang.

The points can be located easily, as most of them are submerged in kind of slits, and they are mostly located near the joints. Move the thumb, holding it quite stiffly, in the areas of the body that are in the vicinity of joints, until you feel a dent that reacts to the pressure by vibrating. The vibration ceases in reaction to the pressure.

Beauty points

The "beauty points" are of the utmost importance. Their role is to rehabilitate body parts and help them function. Access to these points is easy, as they are located mainly in the under areas of the arms, the legs, and the face.

It is important to point out that the yin points, which are the passive, receptive points, are responsible for the body's serenity and for the release of tension, while the yang points, which are the active points, are responsible for increasing the amount of energy and for sexual performance.

The massage of the "beauty points" in the body accomplishes the following:

It enhances the strength of the body.
It increases the energy in the body.
It restores the sparkle to the eyes.
It refreshes the body and creates a feeling of youthfulness.
It smoothes and softens the skin.
It improves the shape of the body.

It releases centers of tension.
It enhances sexual activity and responses.
It improves the voice, giving it a clear resonance.
It improves the function and appearance of the breasts.

The 24 beauty points

We will now explain each of the 24 central "beauty points" in the body. Note that some of the points are in fact "clusters" of points (such as the ones that are located next to the ears - three on each side, totaling six points that are defined as one beauty point). Note also that the points on the arms, palms, feet, and so on, are "double," that is, they appear both on the left and right sides of the body.

The diagrams accompanying all the beauty points will help you identify the location of each one.

The location of beauty point number 1

This is a yang point, and is located on the outer side of the elbow, in the direction of the shoulder. As it is a yang point, it is active, and massaging it relieves toothache, pains in the shoulders, menstrual cramps, and sore and inflamed throats.

Pressure should be exerted on the point, using the thumb. The pressure can be increased by using both thumbs back-to-back. Release. Repeat the action several times.

The location of beauty point number 2

This is a yin point, and is located below the elbow on the inner side of the arm, in the direction of the hand. Massaging this point relieves coughs, helps fight cold symptoms, and alleviates the pain of hemorrhoids.

Gentle but constant pressure should be exerted for a few seconds on the point, using the third finger. Release. Repeat the action several times.

The location of beauty point number 3

This is a yin point, and is located in the center of the inner side of the arm, between the elbow and the palm. Massaging this point eases and regulates the heart rate, and releases stress and pressures caused by nerves and tension.

Gentle but constant pressure should be exerted for a few seconds on the point, using the third finger. Release. Repeat the action several times.

The location of beauty point number 4

This is a yin point, and is located in the middle of the wrist. Massaging this point eases and regulates the heart rate, releases stress and pressures, promotes peaceful, stress-free sleep, and facilitates digestive processes.

Gentle but constant pressure should be exerted for a few seconds on the point, using the third finger. Release. Repeat the action several times.

The location of beauty point number 5

This is a yang point, and is located on the outer edge of the palm, on the thumb side. Massaging this point relieves pains in the fingers, and helps the body expel waste products.

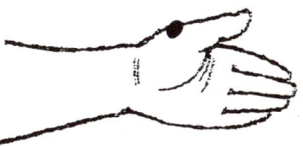

Pressure should be exerted on the point, using the thumb. The pressure can be increased by using both thumbs back-to-back. Release. Repeat the action several times.

The location of beauty point number 6

This is a yang point, and is located on the outer edge of the palm, on the pinkie side. Massaging this point relieves vertigo, headaches, toothaches and pains in the ribs.

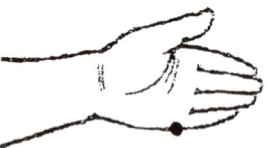

Pressure should be exerted on the point, using the thumb. The pressure can be increased by using both thumbs back-to-back. Release. Repeat the action several times.

The location of beauty point number 7

This is a yang point of great importance, and is located on the outer side of the palm, where the arm is joined to the palm, below the pinkie. Massaging this point promotes good vision.

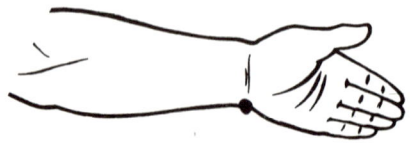

Pressure should be exerted on the point, using the thumb. The pressure can be increased by using both thumbs one on top of the other. Release. Repeat the action several times.

The location of beauty point number 8

This is a yin point, and is located on the sole of the foot, in the fold that is situated below the place between the base of the big toe and the base of the second toe. This is a global point that influences the entire body; its influence is not just localized. This point should therefore be massaged in conjunction with other points in the vicinity. People who suffer from fatigue and exhaustion stemming from insufficient energy to activate the body systems should have this point massaged.

This massage also improves hearing, relieves pains in the kidneys, and helps lower high blood pressure.

Gentle but constant pressure should be exerted for a few seconds on the point, using the thumb or three fingers. Release. Repeat the action.

The location of beauty point number 9

This is a yang point, and is located in the outer edge of the baby toe, in the fold between the toe and the bone at the side. Massaging this point, in addition to improving the characteristics of beauty, helps relieve menstrual cramps, constriction in the heart, stomach-aches, and pains deriving from stones in the gallbladder.

Pressure should be exerted on the point, using the thumb, as well as both thumbs back-to-back. Release. Repeat the action several times.

The location of beauty point number 10
This is a yin point, and is located in the indentation between the lower edge of the big toe and the bone that continues from it, on the sole of the foot. Massaging this point, in addition to its being a beauty point, improves the condition of the eyes, relieves liver and digestive problems, releases tension, and enhances sexual function.

Gentle but constant pressure should be exerted on the point, using the thumb. Release. Repeat the action several times.

The location of beauty point number 11

This is a yang point, and is located on the outer side of the ankle, in the indentation behind the ankle bone. Massaging this point, in addition to its being a beauty point, encourages sexual activity, and eases pains in the legs, hips and lower back. Moreover, the massage releases tensions from the body, alleviates vertigo and headaches, promotes stability in the feet, and relieves pains in the joints and rheumatism, as well as lowering high blood pressure.

Pressure should be exerted on the point, using the thumb. The pressure can be increased by using both thumbs back-to-back. Release. Repeat the action several times.

The location of beauty point number 12

This is a yin point, and is located on the inner side of the leg, at a distance of three finger-widths above the ankle. Massaging this point enhances sexual activity.

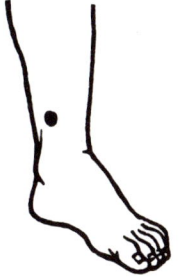

Gentle but constant pressure should be exerted on the point, using the thumb. Release. Repeat the action several times.

The location of beauty point number 13

This is a yin point, and is located on the inner side of the leg, below the knee. Massaging this point increases sexual activity, relieves digestive problems and alleviates difficulties in urination. In addition, it reinforces the knees and hips, loosens and invigorates the body, and increases the amount of energy in the body.

Gentle pressure should be exerted on the point, using the thumb. Release. Repeat the action several times.

The location of beauty point number 14

This is a yang point, and is located on the outer side of the leg, below the knee. Massaging this point, which is global, like point number 8, must be done in conjunction with the rest of the points in the vicinity. The massage increases fertility, bolsters health, and improves the digestive system. It increases the rate of blood circulation, releases stress and tension, and soothes the nerves.

Pressure should be exerted on the point, using the thumb. The pressure can be increased by using both thumbs one on top of the other. Release. Repeat the action several times.

The location of beauty point number 15

This is a yin point, and is located at the meeting point of three yin meridians in the lower region of the leg, at a distance of three finger-widths above the inner side of the ankle. Massaging this point is easy to do, and can therefore be done while working.

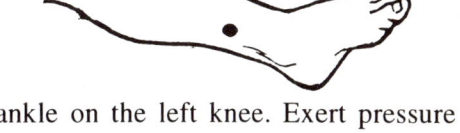

Rest the right ankle on the left knee. Exert pressure on the point for several seconds, using the middle finger of the right hand. Release. Repeat the action several times. Relax.

Rest the left ankle on the right knee. Exert pressure on the point for several seconds, using the middle finger of the left hand. Release. Repeat the action several times.

Now we will deal with the massage points on the head. The aim of massaging these points is to soothe tensions, increase the rate of blood circulation, and restore youthfulness and invigoration.

The location of beauty point number 16

These are in fact two yang points, and they are located at the upper end of the spine, in the place where it joins the skull, at the back of the head (on the slope of the nape). Massaging these points helps dispel tension and relaxes the head muscles, in addition to improving the clarity and deep resonance of the voice.

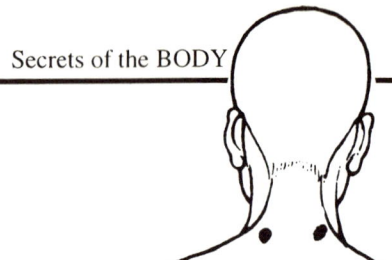

Massaging these points is performed like the massage of yang points in the hands: Exert pressure, using the thumb; release; repeat the action.

The location of beauty point number 17

These are two yang points, and are located on the bones behind and below the ear, on the edges of the nape. Massaging these points improves the hearing and helps stabilize the head.

Massaging these points is performed like the massage of yang points in the hands: exert pressure, using the thumb, release, repeat the action.

The location of beauty point number 18

This is a yang point which is connected to the yang meridian that runs the length of the spinal column. The point is located at the center of the base of the skull, between points number 16. Massaging this point improves the excretion of perspiration, increases the rate of blood circulation, helps reduce excess weight, or maintain an ideal weight. In addition, the massage is responsible for regulating the actions of the body, and in this capacity, has a global function that is of particular importance.

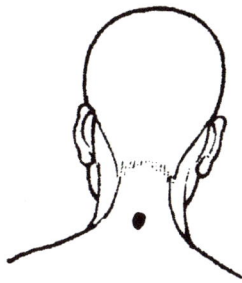

Pressure should be exerted on the point, using the thumb. The pressure can be increased by using both thumbs one on top of the other. Pressure can also be exerted by means of circular movements, in order to release tension and nerves. Release. Repeat the action.

The location of beauty point number 19

This is a yang point of cardinal importance, and it is located on the top of the head. This point can release blockages in the body's systems. It is also a global point, and massaging it improves the functioning of the entire body, increases the rate of blood circulation, and releases tension caused by blockages in the body.

The pressure exerted during the massage is different in adults than in children. In children, the top of the head is not solid enough, and the point must be pressed gently. This is not the case with adults, whose heads are much harder at the top.

Pressure should be exerted for a few seconds, using the middle finger. This can be done using circular movements in the direction of the back of the head in order to dispel tensions. Release. Repeat the action several times.

There are several points on the face which, if they are massaged, can dispel tensions, make pressure lines disappear, ease and brighten tired eyes, freshen up the appearance of the face, and enhance sexual function. This massage should be performed after cleansing the face, using creams or cosmetics as necessary.

The location of beauty point number 20
This is the massage of the forehead. Two of the four points on the forehead are located in the upper part of the forehead, one on each side, near the bones of the forehead, and the two others are located a bit lower, in the indentations between the eyebrows and the bone of the forehead in the direction of the nose. Massaging these points relieves headaches, and releases tension and fatigue from the eyes.

Pressure should be exerted for three seconds, using the middle finger. Release. Repeat the action several times.

The location of beauty point number 21

This is the massage of the eyes. In each eye, there are four meeting points. Two are located at the inner and outer corners of the eye, where the eyelids join, and the other two are located above and below the center of the eye. Massaging these points relieves the eyes of pain, fatigue and strain.

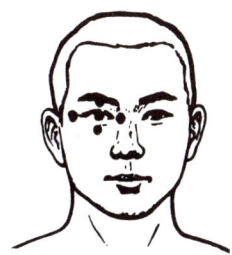

How to massage the points at the corners of the eye, where the eyelids join:

The pressure exerted on the eye must be decreased.

Pressure should be exerted gently but constantly on the points for a few seconds, using the middle finger. Release. Repeat the action several times.

How to massage the points above and below the eye:

Close the eyelids.

Place three fingers on the eyelids without exerting pressure.

Exert light pressure on the center of the eyelid for three seconds, using the pinkie only. Release. Repeat the action several times.

The location of beauty point number 22

This is the massage of the ears. The three points in the ears are located in a straight line, with the first level with the top of the ear, at a distance of a finger-width from the ear in the direction of the face, the second below it, in the indentation that is found at the upper edge of the fold of the lobe inside the hollow of the ear, and the third below it, at the lower edge of the lobe inside the hollow of the ear. Massaging these points enhances the hearing, and prevents a slack jaw.

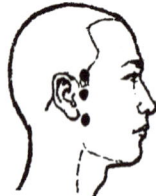

Pressure should be exerted on these points for a few seconds, using the third finger. Release. Repeat the action several times.

The location of beauty point number 23

This is the massage of the nose. In the nose, there are three points, the first of which is located at the lower tip of the nose, in the area between the nostrils and the upper lip. This point is connected to sexuality, and for this reason, the ancient Chinese theory calls it "the center of life." Massaging this point releases tension and nerves, increases the rate of sexual activity, and soothes the region of the nose and mouth.

The other two points are located in the indentation that is behind the edge of the nostrils farthest from the center of the nose. Massaging these points eases breathing, releases stress and tension, and improves the sense of smell.

How to massage the lower tip of the nose:
Pressure should be exerted on this point for a few seconds, using the middle finger. Release. Repeat the action several times.

How to massage the edges of the nostrils:
Pressure should be exerted on these points for a few seconds, using the middle finger. Release. Repeat the action several times.

The location of beauty point number 24
This is the massage of the mouth. There are three points on the mouth, the first two of which are located at the outer edges of the lips, and the third in the middle of the lower lip. Massaging the lips prevents their becoming slack, and helps maintain their shape.

Pressure should be exerted on these points for a few seconds, using the middle finger. Release. Repeat the action several times.

Honing the senses

Acute senses are vital for a person's quality of life, as they afford contact with the people around, and enable the person to enjoy external pleasures such as natural sights, listening to music, smelling aromas, examining the different qualities of substances, and seeing his surroundings. The senses also warn against dangers, and make life easier, more enjoyable and of better quality.

As the senses become dull with time, or as a result of an illness of some kind, it is possible and desirable to improve them and enhance their performance.

In addition, since the senses stem from their connection to particular organs, honing them improves the functioning of the organs that are connected to them. For instance, the ears are connected to the kidneys, the eyes are connected to the liver, the nose to the lungs, the tongue to the heart, the teeth to the stomach, and the lips to the spleen.

The sense of sight - exercising the eyes

Massaging the eyes dispels fatigue and tension in the region of the eyes, improves the quality of vision and the clarity of the reflected image, brightens the whites of the eyes, and strengthens the eye muscles.

1. Rub your hands together to warm them. Close your eyes and place the palms of your hands on them. Remain like this for about half a minute. Open your eyes. Roll your eyes to the left, to the right, up and down. Repeat the exercise several times.

2. Using the middle finger, exert pressure on the inner corner of the eye. Release. Repeat the exercise several times.

Using the middle finger, exert pressure on the outer corner of the eye. Release. Repeat the exercise several times.

3. Close your eyes and place three fingers on the upper part of the eye, with the pinkie on the inner corner of the eye (near the nose).

Exert light pressure with the fingers that are covering the eye. Release.

Move the three fingers to the center of the eye.

Exert light pressure with the fingers that are covering the eye. Release.

Move the fingers to the outer edge of the eye.

Exert light pressure with the fingers that are covering the eye. Release.

Repeat the exercise several times.

The sense of speech - exercising the mouth

Comment: During the course of this exercise, a lot of saliva accumulates in the mouth. According to the ancient Chinese theory, it is the "drug of life." As a result, the saliva must be swallowed slowly during the entire exercise in order not to waste it.

1. Stick your tongue out as far as it will go. Roll it back inside the mouth as far as possible. Release. Repeat the exercise several times.

2. The aim of this exercise is to make the tongue supple, to strengthen the teeth, and to stimulate the gums.

Pass the tongue across the outer side of the upper teeth.

Pass the tongue across the inner side of the upper teeth.

Pass the tongue across the outer side of the lower teeth.

Pass the tongue across the inner side of the lower teeth.

Pass the tongue across the upper gums.
Pass the tongue across the lower gums.

The sense of hearing - exercising the ears

The ears are used for hearing, and among other things produce the wax that provides moisture, preserves the cleanliness of the ears, and improves the quality of hearing.

1. Exert pressure on each of the three points of the ears (number 22).

2. Insert the fourth finger into the hollow of the ear, and with the middle finger, press on the bone behind the ear.

The second finger should be placed above the third, and slid back and forth along it.

Release. Repeat the exercise several times.

Insert the fourth finger into the ear. Pull it out quickly. Repeat the exercise several times.

Bathing - water massage

The Chinese spend a lot of time in the bath, and some of them bathe twice or three times a week.

The hot bath

The hot bath originated in China. The Japanese adopted it later on, and it reached the West more recently.

The theory underlying the concept of the bath states that hot water releases pressures, accelerates the rate of metabolism, increases the rate of blood circulation, speeds up hormone action, improves body functioning, makes the skin smooth, and speeds up the process of getting rid of the dead cells in it.

The soothing water provides a massage for the body, and in this way helps balance the body's energies.

Therefore, you should not make do only with showers, but rather take a bath at least twice a week.

Of course, taking a bath is something that is done during your leisure time, and it should be enjoyed. The body should be able to rest and calm down from its daily worries, while body and soul undergo release and therapy.

While taking a bath, the meridians and the beauty points should be massaged; this can be done without assistance. However, if the assistance of another person is required, you should perform the massage directly after the bath in order to get an enhanced reaction, so that the pores of the skin are still open, the skin is clean and the treatment more effective.

To improve the quality of bathing, the Chinese add the following substances to the bath: natural oils and perfumes, such as lemon, orange, or tangerine peel, pine needles, milk or honey, sea salt, bicarbonate of soda, cornstarch, aromatic herbs such as basil, rosemary and mint. However, modern substances such as bath salts, oils and conditioners, as well as various massages, are effective substitutes.

The soothing bath

This bath can be taken in lukewarm or cold water, and its aim is to give the body pleasure, and to provide it with a sensual experience.

If we want to bathe in hot water, when it is cold outside, or before going to sleep, the water must be very hot, but not boiling, and hot water should be added all the time, in order to maintain the high temperature. The bathroom should also be heated.

In summer, when we want to cool the body, we should bathe in a cool bath, when the water is at a slightly lower temperature than body temperature. Lying in a cool bath for about 12 minutes will give the body a fresh feeling for hours.